FIRST LADIES
OF GARDENING

FIRST LADIES OF GARDENING

PIONEERS, DESIGNERS AND DREAMERS

F

FRANCES LINCOLN LIMITED
PUBLISHERS

HEIDI HOWCROFT
PHOTOGRAPHS BY MARIANNE MAJERUS

CONTENTS

FOREWORD

Classic English gardens full of flowers still hold a fascination for many garden owners and represent what they aspire to, whether they live in the city, suburbs or countryside. A glance through the gardens described in the Yellow Book, published annually by the National Gardens Scheme, soon proves the enduring attraction of the traditional. The English garden has also become something of an export commodity – a phenomenon of which the English themselves remain largely unaware. Foreign visitors come to the RHS Chelsea Flower Show in London not in search of the new but largely for reassurance that the tried-and-tested English flower garden is still alive, well and treasured. Americans and Australians, not to mention the French, Italians, and even Germans, excel at sleek, innovative design, as confirmed by the gardens and houses shown in magazines such as *Architectural Digest* or *Côté Sud*. What these garden fans understandably hanker

after is the secret of the controlled haphazard look, the lightness of touch and the effortless flair that characterize English country gardens.

Admiration for the natural-meets-styled look can be traced back several centuries. During the latter part of the eighteenth and first half of the nineteenth century, the English landscape garden was considered the ultimate in garden design. Royal houses and noble families across Europe swept aside their formal gardens, fountains and sculptures, to replace them with naturalistic landscapes complete with lakes, winding paths, hillocks and dells. The end of the nineteenth and early twentieth century witnessed the rise of the Arts and Crafts Movement, a period characterized by its idealization of English rural life as a contented milieu of cottages and country lanes, hedgerows and meadows. Large country houses were designed to resemble oversized

The double flower borders in the unusual semi-walled garden at Sleightholmedale Lodge (see page 140).

cottages and surrounded by correspondingly romantic gardens conjuring up a reassuringly old-fashioned world and offering an escape from the changes brought about by industry and technology.

After the Second World War, people's tastes turned towards more modern styles. The garden became an extension of the living space, vegetables were bought in supermarkets rather than grown at home, and importance was placed on contemporary building materials while bedding plants and romantic touches were considered passé. However, the euphoric march of progress did not extend as far as the hinterland of the English counties. Deep in the countryside priorities do, after all, differ from those in the big cities and change is often viewed with distrust. People continue to garden here in much the same way as they have always done, ignoring trends and suiting themselves.

The 1980s and early 1990s saw a renaissance of interest in the English flower garden. The economy was booming, people had money to invest in their gardens, and no matter how large or small the plot, whether in the town or countryside, a sense of nostalgia prevailed for the old, familiar type of flower-filled cottage garden. During these two decades an influential role was played by the gardening books emerging from this book's publisher, Frances Lincoln. Well written and lavishly illustrated with enticing photographs, these books could be found on bookshelves, on coffee tables and frequently even on bedside tables up and down the country. They were avidly studied and the plant compositions illustrated inside were eagerly copied.

At the head of this revival were Rosemary Verey and Penelope Hobhouse, whose gardens represented the complete opposite of all that was functional, modern and low-maintenance. Pursuing their own personal tastes, they understood that a garden, like good wine, needs time to develop. Their creations were romantic, overflowing with plants, quintessentially English in style and also supremely photogenic. Anyone who was able to do so visited Barnsley House, Rosemary Verey's masterpiece near Cirencester in the Cotswolds, or went to Somerset in the south-west, where Penelope Hobhouse achieved miracles at Tintinhull Manor. Frances Lincoln, whose contribution to the garden world is greatly underrated, successfully tuned in to the needs of the gardening public and persuaded Rosemary Verey and Penelope Hobhouse to write about their gardens. These two women raised the bar and people could scarcely wait to read their latest publications.

Neither Rosemary Verey nor Penelope Hobhouse would ever have claimed that their style of gardening was easy. On the contrary, they always made it clear how much detailed care and extensive knowledge was involved. Placing the correct plant in a suitable spot at the right time is no simple task. Looking after plants properly and achieving an outwardly effortless and informal appearance requires a range of skills that cannot be acquired overnight, as Beatrice Havergal understood when she founded Waterperry Horticultural School in the 1930s. Juggling with the seasons is another consideration, as is making the most of England's prevailing maritime climate: temperatures are moderate, rain is considered virtually inevitable and, thanks to what are usually relatively short winters, plants enjoy a fairly long growing season. The landscape also plays a decisive role in the look of gardens. Having no vast expanses like America's central plains, no great mountain ranges like the Rockies or the Alps, England's landscapes vary within a comparatively short distance of each other. Each county has a distinct character, providing a wealth of opportunities to produce individual gardens that are in tune with their surroundings.

This book began as a celebration of English gardens that Marianne Majerus and I liked and admired, gardens made in the traditional mould by passionate amateurs. We were looking for gardens created during the second half of the twentieth century, private gardens initially intended for personal use alone and not designed by a third party. We were also keen to focus attention on plants and the skills needed to care for them, since this important aspect of gardening is becoming increasingly marginalized by the trend for instant gardens. As we compiled our shortlist we realized that our favourites were predominantly created or maintained by women. We wanted to talk to the women involved, learn what had inspired and motivated them, so as to appreciate how these unique gardens had come into being.

In a book of this kind it would be impossible not to include Sissinghurst. We also recognize the importance – and not purely in historical terms – of Gertrude Jekyll's work. We were delighted to include Upton Grey Manor with the opportunity to showcase Rosamund Wallinger's achievements. Since both Beth Chatto and Mary Keen continue to make an outstanding contribution to English gardens, it was important to gain an insight into their approach to gardening. Whether exceptional gardens can or should be preserved and developed after the lifetime of their creators is a much discussed question, and this forms a further strand in the book. Barnsley House, East Lambrook Manor, Kiftsgate Court and Helmingham Hall offer us interesting examples of how subsequent generations and new owners are successfully dealing with such a legacy.

We felt it was important not just to present famous gardens but to include newer, lesser-known gardens and also demonstrate how amateur gardeners such as Gill Richardson, Rosanna James, Sue Whittington and Rachel James have managed to create wonderful gardens in some extremely challenging sites. In the mix of exciting gardens rooted in the traditional concept of English gardens we could not ignore what is happening in Ireland and felt we had to include Helen Dillon's garden in our book. After all, there is not just a single type of English garden but a diverse range of alternatives. Although we did not set out to find first ladies of gardening, we nevertheless found them: inspirational women who are passionate about the quintessential English garden.

Heidi Howcroft and Marianne Majerus, London

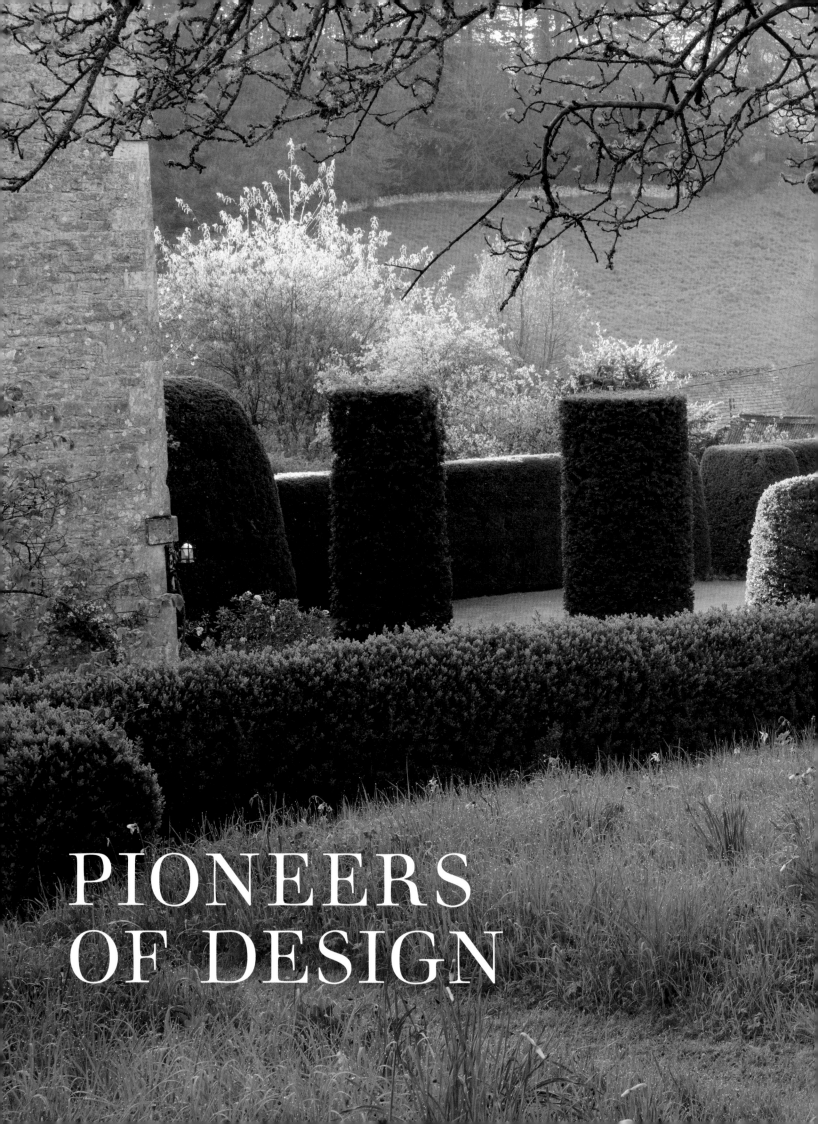

PIONEERS
OF DESIGN

ROSAMUND WALLINGER

JEKYLL'S RESTORED MASTERPIECE

How Upton Grey Manor was brought back to life

Upton Grey is one of those English villages untouched by time which remains steeped in tradition. It is perhaps fitting, therefore, that it was here, abutting the church and surrounded by trees, that an English garden masterpiece managed to remain hidden from sight for several decades. This garden which had been created during the heyday of English gardens was reawakened from its long slumbers by a remarkable woman named Rosamund Wallinger. The garden was, in fact, low on the list of the Wallingers' priorities when they bought Upton Grey. What they were mainly looking for was a house in the country within commuting distance of London where they could park their car in peace, as John Wallinger had become tired of the habitual evening hunt for a parking space at the end of a long working day. To begin with, his wife Rosamund thought it was all a bit of a hare-brained scheme that would eventually be forgotten. However, thirty years on, Rosamund Wallinger, who once had only a tiny garden in London to care for and had no interest either in plants or gardens, is now usually found in the middle of a flower bed with a pair of secateurs in hand.

ACCIDENTAL DISCOVERY

This perfect image of an English lady gardener did not develop overnight. Nor was it ever intended: it was all the fault of the house, Upton Grey Manor, and the result of a brief, almost incidental entry in records discovered in the library of the Royal Institute of British Architects. These documented that the house was a listed building and that the garden was believed to have been designed by Gertrude Jekyll (1843–1932). With no real idea of what she was letting herself in for, Rosamund Wallinger immersed herself in the world of garden archaeology. Her investigations were to involve years of detective work, frustration, determination and back-breaking graft, all of which were ultimately rewarded by immense pleasure. Rosamund Wallinger succeeded in restoring a garden designed by the most significant female gardener in the history of English gardens. Gertrude Jekyll designed the garden from 1908–09 as an extension to the house which had been built, or rather rebuilt, by Ernest Newton for publisher Charles Holme (1848–1923).

The garden of Upton Grey Manor in Hampshire, not far from Basingstoke, is exquisite. It has been restored to its original state right down to the last shrub. Today, it represents the story of two women, the expert and the novice. Rosamund Wallinger recorded her journey of discovery – which is the only way to describe the way she tackled this garden project – in two books: in 2000, she published *Gertrude Jekyll's Lost Garden* and in 2013 she produced her most recent work, *Gertrude Jekyll: Her Art Restored*

at Upton Grey. Both volumes are in the form of an album and document the step-by-step process of how the garden was revealed and developed. When the Wallingers first viewed the house in 1983, their attention was focused on the historic building. The 2 hectares/5 acres of garden – as far as it could even be described as a garden – was a wilderness, an unkempt jungle of blackberry bushes, shrubs and overhanging trees. A year later, the new owners moved into the house, itself sorely in need of renovation, and began doing some research on the garden, scouring libraries to find clues as to its original state. Their research led them to the University of California, which holds and administers the archives of Beatrix Farrell, known as the Reef Point Collection. This collector, herself an important landscape architect, had purchased all the plans, photographs and albums belonging to Gertrude Jekyll's heirs and amalgamated them for posterity. Part of this treasure included a total of nineteen garden plans for Upton Grey Manor, a complete set of designs which contained all the relevant information, from the measurement plan to the meticulously drawn planting plans, as well as a detailed picture of how the garden eventually looked. In common with other designers of her time, Gertrude Jekyll always kept the originals of her designs, providing her clients with a copy.

PURE JEKYLL

Upton Grey is just one of more than 300 gardens which Jekyll designed in her lifetime. However, it occupies a special position in her life's work: although many gardens claim to be Jekyll gardens, many of them were only partially designed by her. Others have undergone such radical changes over the years that the true art of this outstanding garden designer is no longer in evidence.

Anyone who believes that creativity is the preserve of youth will be obliged to revise this opinion on seeing Upton Grey. Miss Jekyll

was sixty-five when she accepted the commission. While others were already enjoying retirement, she was at the peak of her design career, a line of work that she wandered into by chance. In 1891, a German eye specialist in Wiesbaden, by the name of Pagenstecher, strongly advised her to give up painting and embroidery if she wanted to preserve her sight. She was just fifty-two at the time, a spinster who lived for her art. She was a progressive lady, cultured, well-educated and well-travelled, from a good family and financially secure. Although she lived with her mother, she had a free hand in developing their garden at Munstead in Surrey in her own style. It soon began to attract leading figures from the gardening world. In 1882, when the constant stream of visitors became too much for her mother, Gertrude acquired a plot of adjacent land measuring about six hectares/15 acres on which she created the framework for Munstead Wood Garden. It was here that Gertrude wrote her books and lived until her death at the age of eighty-nine. Another milestone in her life was her meeting in 1889 with Edwin Lutyens (1869–1944), who was then a young man on the threshold of his career as an architect. Their first meeting over afternoon tea was a formal affair. Their second encounter, an invitation to Jekyll's home, left a much stronger impression, as described in Francis Jekyll's book *Gertrude Jekyll: A Memoir*:

> 'Genial and chatty, dressed in a short
> blue skirt that hardly hid her ankles
> and in boots that were made famous by
> W. Nicholson's painting; a blue apron
> with huge kangaroo-like pockets full of
> gardening things; a blue-striped pleated
> blouse with narrow sleeves tight around
> her round wrists, just giving her small
> and distinctive hands freedom to move.'

It marked the beginning of an exceptional partnership, which was to influence the appearance of country houses all over the British Isles. Anyone occupying a Lutyens house with a Jekyll garden had arrived, socially speaking. The pair also developed the ideal of a perfect English country house with long roofs, chimneys, leaded windows, surrounded by a romantic, flower-filled garden, lawned areas for tennis and croquet, room for garden furniture and serving afternoon tea and providing a plentiful supply of cut flowers for the house. Despite looking old on the outside, it had to be comfortable or even 'cottagey' on the inside. No cost was spared to achieve what was then considered a modern lifestyle. The English country house style was born and the vision of living in a cottage became the dream of the growing population of middle classes.

Popular and hard-working as she was, Jekyll designed about ten gardens per year. This was a considerable number considering that everything had to be drawn by hand. In addition, she also wrote newspaper articles and books, which are nowadays regarded as standard references. She set up a nursery for herbaceous plants to supply her architects with the appropriate stock and displayed keen business acumen. Rosamund Wallinger has copies of bills from the Munstead Wood nursery, which include handwritten notes itemizing the quantities, prices and noting whether the goods had been delivered.

GARDENS AS ART

Gertrude Jekyll was an authority on everything to do with gardening and a pioneer of gardens as an art form. However, the 1950s ushered in a new passion for modernism and Gertrude Jekyll became less fashionable. Although her name was still familiar and well respected in professional circles, it was not widely known by the general public. It is not surprising, therefore, that when Rosamund Wallinger came across the name Jekyll, she had no idea who she was dealing with. As she herself admits, she was purely concerned with producing a faithful reconstruction: 'This garden is a recreation of Jekyll's art, not mine.'

When Rosamund took stock of the garden at Upton Grey, Jekyll's former design was a wilderness. It had to be cleared, dug over and cut back without disturbing the basic elements. Bit by bit, natural stone walls, the outlines of beds, remains of old rose stocks all began to emerge. With the aid of plans, which were kindly

Pergolas, festooned with roses, such as 'Cécile Brünner' shown here, are true hallmarks of a Jekyll garden. The bantam hens are Rosamund's addition and have the run of the entire garden.

Working from the original planting plans, Rosamund Wallinger was able to restock the flower beds.
In the example shown here, she used bearded iris (*Iris germanica*) and peonies such as *Paeonia lactiflora*
'Sarah Bernhardt'.

copied and made available by the Reef Point Collection, the garden slowly revealed itself. The preparation work for this major project was considerable and not to be underestimated. Before any planting could even begin, walls had to be repaired. The project was soon being talked about and gained the attention of the Hampshire Gardens Trust while some valuable tips were offered by experts including Richard Bisgrove and Penelope Hobhouse who visited the building site – no one could describe it as a garden at this stage. Without interfering, they inspired and encouraged Rosamund, an approach which this novice gardener greatly appreciated then as she does now. Consequently, she was able to work at her own pace – a factor which was crucial to her success since despite being in possession of the planting blueprints, this by no means meant that she could get started immediately. The plans first had to be decoded since Gertrude Jekyll's handwriting

was, like her embroidery, meticulous and fine. Thus, Rosamund Wallinger, in addition to all her other newly acquired skills, has become a true expert on Jekyll's handwriting

RAISING FROM SEED

Another challenge was to acquire the plants. Given the quantities required, a large proportion had to be raised from seed, a further steep learning curve for a woman who had started with no basic gardening knowledge. In the process, Rosamund Wallinger has become extremely knowledgeable about sourcing historic plants and constructing pergolas and supports for cascading roses. She studied old photographs made available by former owners of the house and gradually, one bed at a time, the garden has re-emerged. If the garden had been restored by a professional, it would probably have turned out a bit too formal as it would have taken shape too quickly. The finer details

Each area has a different theme, from the Rose Garden on the right, to the diagonal line of the herbaceous border and Rosamund's spectacular 'parking lot for plants', which can be glimpsed behind the yew hedge.

and the character of the setting, both of which define today's garden, would have been lost. Furthermore, it would have been difficult to withstand the temptation to 'improve on' the blueprint. Rosamund Wallinger, on the other hand, followed Gertrude Jekyll's instructions to the letter, not only studying the plans and plant lists but also reading books on the subject in order to gain a better insight into the working environment of her role model.

IN PROPORTION

Gertrude Jekyll's garden at Upton Grey Manor, reawakened by Rosamund Wallinger, is a work of art. It is compact, homely and manageable – an adjective not normally associated with Jekyll's gardens. There is a certain logic which runs through the entire garden area. The periphery of the garden is informal and natural, becoming more formal towards the house. The plans show that Jekyll designed the garden layout without

the help of an architect. Upton Grey Manor provides the proof, if needed, to understand why Gertrude Jekyll's designs were so popular in her lifetime. The garden is fresh, alive and absolutely perfect in its proportions. There are neither endless stretches of ground cover nor flights of steps competing for attention. The greenery and the plants have the final word. Gertrude Jekyll is known for her masterly use of herbaceous beds and her delicately balanced colour combinations. In Upton Grey, however, it is clear that these are just a small part of her contribution to garden art while rose gardens and so-called wild gardens are an equally important element of her repertoire.

The garden is divided into formal and informal areas. Both parts are distinctly different in character yet retain elements common to both, the sense of continuity is largely achieved using roses. The flower-filled Formal Garden with its

Above The Rose Garden is situated at the heart of the garden, a testimony to Miss Jekyll's planning and Rosamund's work.
Below From the upstairs windows of the main house, one can see how the garden is skilfully divided into different areas.

Rose Garden, bowling green, tennis court and herbaceous beds unfolds in terraces at the rear of the house. In front of the house, parallel to the driveway and barely noticeable at first glance, is the Wild Garden, a long rectangular area, almost as large as the Formal Garden. Here, too, the ground is landscaped on different levels. Whereas these levels are retained in the Formal Garden by natural stone supporting walls, the wild area incorporates a slight rise that slopes gently away. These slopes are planted with drifts of daffodils which, along with other wild flowers, are visible from the house as a gentle shimmer of colour in spring. The roses emerge gradually, clusters of small buds which make excellent companions to the lilac and other flowering shrubs. Groups of shrub and rambler roses such as 'The Garland', *Rosa virginiana* and 'Blush Rambler' are modest focal points, as Gertrude Jekyll suggests in her book *Wood and Garden*:

> 'I am strongly for treating garden and
> wooded ground in a pictorial way, mainly
> with large effects, and in the second place,
> with lesser beautiful incidents, and for
> so arranging plants and trees and grassy
> spaces that they look happy and at home,
> and make no parade of conscious effort.'

In accordance with these sentiments, the pond is situated in a secluded spot, its banks surrounded by plants and hidden from view: a place to retreat to after the splendour and show of the Formal Garden.

CHOREOGRAPHED COLOUR

By way of contrast, the Formal Garden is a riot. From May to September it produces a choreographed sequence of wonderful blooms which appear to be entirely visible from the terrace. It is only on closer inspection, however, that one becomes aware of the large number of hidden surprises in the form of all kinds of details, which reflect the careful thought that has gone into planting each area, from the smallest flower bed to a run of natural stone walls. Although the design of the beds and division of space is formal, the planting is informal and varied, giving a certain picturesque quality to the overall effect. A concept of this scale requires enormous experience. The strength of Jekyll's planting lies in her colour schemes which are specially chosen to complement the gentle, milky light of a Hampshire summer. This garden is also the most successful example of how best to integrate a tennis court into a garden. Boasting a lawn that would not look out of place at Wimbledon and, like the rest of the Formal Garden, surrounded by yew hedging, the function of this area is not immediately obvious. Is this thanks to the lawn, which provides a calm, neutral background or to the rose pergola in the middle? Set back into a niche in the hedge and covered with a profusion of roses, including 'Paul's Himalayan Musk', this charming pergola is an eye-catching attraction.

PROFUSION AND TRANQUILITY

What makes this garden so charming is the alternate mix of profusion and tranquility. The geometrical beds of the Rose Garden, cut out of a lawned area, not only contain roses such as 'Madame Caroline Testout' and 'Killarney', but are also bordered by peonies (*Paeonia officinalis* 'Lize van Veen'), and lilies (*Lilium regale*), as well as lambs' tongue (*Stachys byzantina*). Slightly raised on the surrounding, almost horseshoe-shaped area are the herbaceous beds, also called mixed borders. These are numbered as are all the beds shown on the plan. They contain daylilies, asters, lupins and many others, too many to list individually. Dahlias, which Gertrude Jekyll liked to use as fillers to disguise faded plants, can be seen during the summer months along with the annuals *Nigella damascena* and cosmos. The diversity is impressive and it must be borne in mind that all this has been accomplished by a woman who is entirely self-taught. There is a gardener, as well as occasional part-time staff who work in the garden, but only as helpers. Rosamund Wallinger carries out the bulk of the work herself.

Skilful placing of green-leaved shrubs is particularly useful for bringing out the luminescent, pale colours of the roses, peonies and lilies.

The knowledge and skills required to maintain a Jekyll garden, let alone plant it, are considerable. It is only by looking at the photographs displayed in the conservatory and comparing them with how the garden looks today that one can fully appreciate the incredible achievements of this slim, delicate woman. Rosamund's husband, who was essentially the root cause for all this, works in the background, supporting his wife, sacrificing his weekends and taking an energetic part in the clearance operations. Just how far Rosamund Wallinger has come in terms of gardening is evident from the Kitchen Garden which she has planted at the side of the house. Here, parallel to the Formal Garden and, from an outsider's perspective, an integral part of Gertrude Jekyll's overall composition, is where her stock plants live. Right at the end are also a few vegetables and kitchen herbs for daily use. This area, with Jekyll-style double herbaceous borders, which lead to cascading rose arbours with an apple orchard beyond, could easily have been designed by Gertrude Jekyll as the beds clearly echo the hallmarks of her style of planting. It was in fact designed by her long-standing pupil Rosamund Wallinger.

VISUAL DELIGHT

Jekyll's gardens are a visual delight, often characterized by tiny, yet crucial details. While restoring the garden, a decision was made to dispense with a little supporting wall, barely 30cm/12in high, between the tennis court and bowling green, and to allow the ground to slope down instead. At first Rosamund Wallinger herself did not realize the importance of this tiny wall until she saw the cover of her first book. The slope was certainly in place but the crisp outline, the dotting of the 'i', was missing and the composition lacked balance. This finishing touch has now been reinstated. Delicate and unobtrusive, a narrow bed at the base of the little wall now not only outlines the lawn area but also defines the flowing descent of the terraces and – even more importantly – creates a sense of depth.

The gardens of Upton Grey Manor are an inspiration. With Rosamund Wallinger as a role model and Gertrude Jekyll as a teacher, it is possible with enough determination for any one of us to create an English garden masterpiece on our doorstep.

GUIDING PRINCIPLES

❋ 'The love of gardening is a seed that once sown never dies, but grows and grows to an enduring and ever-increasing source of happiness.' Gertrude Jekyll, *Wood and Garden* (1899).

❋ 'Let no one be discouraged by the thought of how much there is to learn.' Apposite words from the introduction to *Wood and Garden*, which Rosamund Wallinger took to heart. Intensive research and preparation cannot be avoided when working on historical projects.

❋ If an original plant is not available, one must improvise.

❋ The value of annuals as fillers in a flower bed should not be underestimated. One of the best old-fashioned species in this respect is the much-neglected snapdragon (*Antirrhinum*).

SIGNATURE PLANTS

❋ Peonies such as *Paeonia lactiflora* 'Sarah Bernhardt' and *P. officinalis* (top image).

❋ Delphiniums in the herbaceous borders and in the 'plant parking lot' bed; here, *Delphinium elatum*. (2nd image from top.)

❋ Irises (*Iris pallida* and *I. germanica*). Almost all the varieties mentioned by Gertrude Jekyll on her plan have now been lost to cultivation. Consequently, modern equivalents such as 'Sable' and 'Golden Harvest' have been used instead. More modest varieties, such as *Iris pseudacorus* (3rd image from top) have been used in the Wild Garden.

❋ Rambler roses, such as 'Blush Noisette' (4th image from top) and climbing 'Blush Rambler' (introduced in 1903). Rosamund believes that Jekyll's favourite was 'The Garland', a rose which is also one of her own favourites.

❋ Fragrant daylily (*Hemerocallis dumortieri*) with a long flowering season. *Bergenia cordifolia*, frequently used by Miss Jekyll as an edging plant for flower beds.

'This garden is a recreation of Jekyll's art, not mine.'
Rosamund Wallinger

VITA SACKVILLE-WEST

(1892–1962)

VITA'S LIFEWORK AT SISSINGHURST

The genesis of an exceptional garden

For many garden lovers, Sissinghurst Castle Garden in Kent represents the height of perfection. It has become a place of pilgrimage and thousands of gardening enthusiasts visit each year to experience it at first hand. However, given the crowds that throng the garden at peak season, it is unlikely that conditions are ideal for visitors to sense the true spirit of the place, which goes deeper than a collection of outstanding plant compositions.

People often wonder what it is that sets Sissinghurst Castle Garden apart from other remarkable gardens and why, more than fifty years after the death of its creator, it still possesses such a powerful attraction. The secret of Sissinghurst's success lies in the fact that it is inseparably linked to the lives and attitudes of Vita Sackville-West and her husband Harold Nicolson. Vita herself would be astonished, and possibly even horrified, to know that she is now no longer famous for her literary works, including *The Land* (1926) and other poems, and books such as *The Edwardians* (1930), but for her garden and what she called her 'beastly little *Observer* articles', which were later published in book form and became a bestseller. Writing was her passion, while the garden gave her a sense of balance. To some extent, Sissinghurst is like an album of memories and reflects the subjects that preoccupied Vita as an author: the countryside and love.

KNOLE CHILDHOOD

In defiance of the customs of the day, Vita Sackville-West retained her maiden name all her life, not only because of her work as a writer but, more importantly, because of her sense of pride in belonging to an aristocratic family steeped in tradition. The fact that as a woman she was not entitled to inherit Knole House, where she was born and which had been home to the Sackville family since 1603, was a source of great sadness to her all her life. It was reminders of Knole that she sought and found in Sissinghurst. During her childhood she had the run of the 300-room property, which was located near Sevenoaks, in Kent, and radiated history from every wall. The garden at Knole, extending over about 10 hectares/25 acres, was a private, magical world where this independently minded little girl would have loved to play just as she pleased, were it not for the watchful eye of the strict head gardener who guarded this particular kingdom.

Born in 1892 and baptized Victoria Mary Sackville-West, she was an only child and

The garden in front of South Cottage, filled with yellow kniphofias, verbascum and the daisy heads of *Inula helenium*, represents a sophisticated version of the cottage-garden style.

was called Vita to distinguish her from her beautiful and overbearing mother, Lady Victoria Sackville. As the daughter of a lord, Vita, like other young ladies of the era, was introduced into society. The many love affairs in which her parents indulged left her disillusioned about marriage and what she yearned for most was a companionable relationship that would make her happy. *Vita: The Life of Vita Sackville-West*, the prize-winning biography by Victoria Glendinning, provides an outstanding insight into the personal journey and complicated life of this exceptional woman, who seems to have been constantly in search of love and recognition. All this is of great significance in the story of Sissinghurst Castle and its garden, for in Harold Nicolson, a diplomat six years her senior, Vita found a man with whom she could share her life. Their marriage was far from conventional. They both had numerous friendships and relationships, but were united

by the gardens at Sissinghurst, which provided them with a common bond.

THE LONG BARN EXPERIENCE

Sissinghurst was not the family's first garden. Their early knowledge and initial experience came from Long Barn (a few kilometres south of Knole), where they lived from 1915 to 1930. They were visited here by the famous and highly respected architect, Edwin Lutyens, a friend of Vita's mother, who gave them much helpful advice on creating terraces. In 1917 Lutyens introduced Vita and her mother to Gertrude Jekyll. They went to see Jekyll at her home in Munstead Wood, Surrey, and Vita recorded in her notebook that she was impressed by the garden. She went on to introduce at Sissinghurst many of the same roses that grew in Jekyll's garden. Writer Jane Brown examines this and other influences in her book entitled *Vita's Other World*.

Old-fashioned 'Henry Eckford' sweet peas, lupins and roses around the front door add their charm to the pastoral mood.

Each of the garden enclosures at Sissinghurst has its own theme, yet all share a sense of structure and great attention to detail, as illustrated here in the Herb Garden.

END OF AN IDYLL

In 1930, Harold took the difficult decision of retiring from the diplomatic service in order to work as a journalist. That same year, their idyll at Long Barn came to an end: the property next door was sold with the intention of converting it into a chicken farm. Their search for a new home did not take long, however. In April 1930 a friend had told them of a sixteenth-century castle for sale in Kent. It sounded wonderful, but in reality was a collection of separate buildings around a central tower, surrounded by brick walls. The buildings were in a desperate state of neglect. Vita described her first impressions in the *Journal of the Royal Horticultural Society* published in November 1953:

'Yet the place, when I first saw it on a summer
day in 1930, caught instantly at my heart and
my imagination. I fell in love: love at first
sight. I saw what might be made of it. It was
Sleeping Beauty's Castle; but a castle running

away into sordidness and squalor; a garden crying out for rescue.'

Vision and courage were required to take on such a project. Vita had both. In addition to the purchase price of around £12,000, Harold would need to spend a further £15,000 just to make the buildings habitable. They wondered whether it would not be more prudent to buy a new house. But Vita was charmed by the romantic atmosphere, the tower had certain architectural similarities with her beloved Knole, and Harold had also meanwhile discovered that the place had been occupied in the early sixteenth century by a member of the Sackville family. That settled matters and Sissinghurst was brought back to life.

MOVING ON

Photographs taken during the 1930s show just how much work had to be done. To the right and

The tower provides an excellent view of the network of paths that cleverly links the garden's different areas. The yew-hedge Rondel occupies a key point in the centre and forms an oasis of tranquility.

left of the walled-up entrance stretched a row of houses. Behind this was the tower, while on opposite boundaries stood the Priest's House and the South Cottage. Between and abutting the buildings was an area of 4 hectares/ 10 acres: grass around the tower, a kitchen garden, walls, an overgrown apple orchard, and along the outer edge of the property the remains of a moat.

The unusual arrangement of buildings seemed to perfectly suit the family's lifestyle. Each family member, including sons Ben and Nigel, had their own private space, in addition to shared rooms where the family could spend time together. The tower was Vita's study and library. The boys were allotted the Priest's House, which also incorporated the family kitchen and dining room on the ground floor. South Cottage housed Vita and Harold's bedroom, as well as an office for Harold.

Household staff were accommodated next to the main entrance, but guest rooms and a family living room were not included in the plans. In order to get from one living space to another, there was nothing for it but to brave the wind and weather and cross the open area outside. The family did not move into the property until 1932. Money was in short supply and Harold had difficulty earning a living in his new field of work. Vita, inspired by the challenges which Sissinghurst presented, was busily involved with her writing.

HAROLD'S OVERVIEW

Sissinghurst is often regarded as all Vita's work but Harold's role should not be forgotten. It was he, after all, who gave the garden its structure and shape. He designed a good deal of the layout from up in the tower, which gave him a good view over the property. He took care of all the measuring up and marked out the different sections with string and posts. In the ongoing battle with irregular shapes – no building was at true right angles to another – he decided to site roughly square-shaped areas in front of the Priest's House and South Cottage. The old kitchen garden was divided into sections and criss-crossed with formal paths. Main axes, such as the Yew Walk and Moat Walk, were important routes in day-to-day life. A good deal of careful planning was necessary and the whole project took ten years to complete. The gardens in front of South Cottage and the Priest's House were laid out in a cruciform pattern. The Lime Walk, created in 1932, connected the nuttery with the herb garden and kitchen garden. The Rondel, a circular yew hedge that forms one of the garden's main features, was not planted until 1937. The idea for the White Garden was first conceived in 1939 but the plans were put on hold for ten years.

This organic development is what makes Sissinghurst special. Had enough money been available to carry out the project in one go, the end result might have been less successful. The sequence of walls and hedges, bisecting lines and vistas defining individual areas make the garden a compelling experience. And although these individual areas were designed to meet particular requirements, they nonetheless merge into a harmonious and satisfying whole.

VITA'S ROUTINE

Anyone wishing to retrace Vita's daily route should start from her study in the tower, then make their way first to South Cottage and then the Priest's House. Not surprisingly, Vita grew very familiar with the plants she passed on her way, observing them at different times of day and in every season. The plants continue to play the same important role in the garden as in Vita's day. They lend colour, texture and scent to soften the solidity and angularity of the brickwork. A delicate, deeply romantic note characterizes the entire garden. Harold may have been responsible for the structure, but it was Vita who brought the borders to life. Travelling had awakened Vita's feeling for botany, and visits to other gardens and houses opened up a world of opportunities. As Anne

Scott-James aptly describes in *Sissinghurst: The Making of a Garden*, Vita had access to a higher class of garden, 'for gardening has its own social structure, like everything else'.

In addition to grand estates such Wilton, in Wiltshire, Vita drew inspiration from several more modest sites. She shared a passion for old-fashioned roses with the owner of Kiftsgate Court (see page 92), Heather Muir. Roses were also one of the main features at East Lambrook Manor garden (see page 48). Tintinhull Garden in Somerset, established by Phyllis Reiss in the 1930s, was another of Vita's great favourites. The two women exchanged planting ideas.

GROWING REPUTATION

Sissinghurst's fame is largely due to Vita's weekly columns for the *Observer*. The articles she wrote for this Sunday newspaper between 1946 and 1960 were practical and entertaining and appealed to the English gardening public. Later on, they were compiled in a series of four books. Vita wrote about her latest discoveries, problems in the garden, and appreciations of plants that she felt were unfairly neglected (such as aquilegias, or the rose 'American Pillar'). Vita, who never claimed to be an expert, wrote from experience. She offered tips on where to source different plants and did not shy away from including the occasional trenchant comment. She was categorical, for example, on the subject of conifers: 'some people like conifers: I, frankly, don't.'

Her readers naturally wanted to see the garden for themselves. Sissinghurst had first opened to the public in 1938 and visitors were known by the family as 'shillingses', in reference to the entry fee. Vita was often present – a tall, striking woman, dressed in knee breeches and boots – and willing to answer questions, which contributed to the charm and character of the garden, and certainly heightened the visitors' experience. Eccentric and outwardly self-assured, Vita had an unmistakably aristocratic bearing. She was invited as a speaker to give talks, abroad as well as in England. Prominent figures, including the Queen Mother, also visited Sissinghurst, adding to the garden's celebrity.

Roses such as 'Blush Rambler' have overrun the old apple trees, enveloping them in a magical, romantic atmosphere. From this perspective, the tower appears taller and more impressive, as if it were part of a much larger estate, and is reminiscent of Knole, Vita's beloved birthplace.

The Lime Walk along the edge of the garden is one of its main axes and was designed by Harold Nicholson. It leads towards one of the statues that adorn Sissinghurst.

The day-to-day work of mowing the lawns, cutting hedges and weeding was taken over by gardeners, while Vita concentrated on her vision for the garden. She experimented with the new and ripped out the old.

Two years before her death in 1962, Vita hired two women gardeners from Waterperry Horticultural School (see page 36). Pamela Schwerdt and Sibylle Kreutzberger, whom Vita simply referred to in German as 'Mädchen', the girls, were largely responsible for the continuity of the garden when it was handed over to the National Trust five years after Vita's death. They maintained the garden for the new owners for another thirty-one years.

What we see today is, of necessity, a pared-down version of the original garden. Space, atmosphere and plants are the outstanding elements of Sissinghurst; it is still beautiful and yet it lacks the individual flair of its creators.

Even with the Nicolson family keeping a custodial eye over the garden, it is difficult to achieve a balance between the crowds of visitors and the personality of the garden.

ROMANCE AT HEART

There is no other garden quite like Sissinghurst. The design can be copied, as can the planting, but not the location or the bygone lifestyle of Vita and Harold. As garden lovers, we have benefited from Harold's ability to give Vita the freedom she needed to develop her talents. Whether in the famous and much-imitated White Garden, under the rose-covered apple trees of the orchard, or in the bright, hot-coloured flower beds outside South Cottage, romance is at the heart of this remarkable garden.

GUIDING PRINCIPLES

❀ Having Sissinghurst and Vita Sackville-West as role models should give us the confidence to landscape our own gardens gradually, over a period of years, to acquire a thorough knowledge of the place and not allow ourselves to be influenced by trends.

❀ When choosing plants, always be open to new ideas, be prepared to experiment and do not be afraid to fill up the space available. Vita was in favour of using every crack and crevice, advocating 'Cram, cram, cram every chink and cranny.' She was convinced that it was more effective to 'plant twelve tulips together rather than to split them into two groups of six'.

❀ A good gardener never stops learning. Vita did not think of herself as an expert, was modest about her achievements and, above all, never shirked hard work.

❀ Anyone wanting to copy Sissinghurst will need an awkward plot of land, dilapidated buildings, a large amount of artistic talent, points of reference to which one can always return for direction, and infinite patience for immersing oneself in the world of gardens.

SIGNATURE PLANTS

❀ Climbing *Rosa mulliganii* (see also pages 26–7; top).

❀ Lilies such as *Lilium regale* or 'Apollo' (2nd image from top).

❀ White tansy (*Achillea ptarmica*) (3rd image from top).

❀ *Delphinium* 'Ice Cap' (4th image from top).

❀ White rosebay willowherb (*Chamaenerion angustifolium* 'Album').

❀ Scotch thistle (*Onopordum*).

❀ *Wisteria brachybotrys* 'Shiro-kapitan'.

'It caught at my heart and my imagination. I fell in love: love at first sight. I saw what might be made of it.'
Vita Sackville-West

MISS HAVERGAL'S GIRLS

Waterperry Horticultural School and the pursuit of excellence

Two factors are crucial for the success of an English flower garden: horticultural know-how and expert care. Only if you have spent decades caring for and developing labour-intensive gardens, accumulating knowledge and expertise in tried-and–tested methods, do you know when and what to do in the garden. Experienced gardeners are rare and it comes as no surprise that such experts are highly sought after. This is not a new phenomenon, but one that Beatrix Havergal sought to address nearly a century ago.

Due to a growing desire among the middle classes at the end of the nineteenth century to surround themselves with impressive, flower-filled gardens, to serve their own fresh fruit and vegetables at table, and to enjoy a perfect English lawn for tennis and croquet, the gardening business experienced a boom. The demand for gardeners was high and even young women from respectable families were becoming interested in the profession. Special schools, such as Swanley Horticultural College in Kent, or Viscountess Wolseley's College of Gardening in Glynde, East Sussex, were established to train 'lady gardeners'. Graduating students were either employed as senior gardeners in the numerous country houses or ran their own establishments as the lady of the house.

ESTABLISHING THE SCHOOL

Although Beatrix Havergal (1901–80) is regarded as one of the key figures of the English garden movement, she is no longer particularly well known in contemporary gardening circles. She pursued her dream of becoming a gardener and trained at Thatcham Fruit and Flower Farm near Newbury, Berkshire. After a two-year apprenticeship she found a position nearby at Downe House girls' school, where she met Avice Sanders who was then the school's housekeeper. Together they longed to create a training school specifically for female gardeners and – despite a shortage of capital at the outset – they succeeded in turning their idea into reality. They knew full well that they would have to start from modest beginnings.

In 1927 the two women rented the Gardener's Cottage, with adjoining garden, from Pusey House in Oxfordshire. It was here that they established their first school, with just two pupils. They intended to provide a practical apprenticeship for young women, to teach them all aspects of garden and vegetable cultivation from the ground up. Home-economy subjects, which were Avice Sanders' area of expertise, were also offered so that students would gain detailed knowledge ranging from sowing seeds and tending plants right through to harvesting and preparing or storing the produce. The women's income was derived from the girls'

Enclosed by a dense yew hedge, the Formal Garden reflects various periods of history. The plant composition, including box, berberis, dahlias and asters, is both original and enchanting.

school fees and from selling vegetables, fruit, cut flowers and young plants. The venture was a success: their training methods met with acclaim and their produce sold well. After just a few years, and despite limited finances, Beatrix Havergal and Avice Sanders began looking for a new and bigger site for their school, one that would provide better accommodation for their students and a larger area to cultivate.

In Waterperry, not far from Oxford, they found the ideal location. The house, which dated back to the twelfth century and had been renovated at the beginning of the nineteenth, was spacious enough to house both dormitories and classrooms. The walled garden, planted with fruit trees, was surrounded by a herbaceous border. A tributary of the River Thames flowed along the edge of the property, ensuring fertile soil. At the end of August 1932, the two women moved into their splendid new home along with six pupils, three members of staff and their dog, James. The move from Gardener's Cottage to this manor house was a giant leap. From the income they gained from selling tomatoes, grapes, other fruit and vegetables, as well as bedding, herbaceous plants and cut flowers, they were able to buy furniture, equipment, wheelbarrows and even a car – much of which came from auctions. Magdalen College in Oxford, as the owner of Waterperry, had, with wise foresight and possibly as a gesture of goodwill towards these young entrepreneurs, fixed a staggered rent for a period of sixteen years: £150 for the first three years, progressively rising to £500 after the sixth year.

CAMARADERIE

Three students who had completed their three-year course before the move decided to stay and help out at the new school. In her book *Waterperry: A Dream Fulfilled*, Ursula Maddy comments that this says a good deal about the affection and sense of camaraderie among the teaching staff. Such was the scale of the project that every bit of help was needed: not only did a large number of plants have to be relocated from Pusey but the new cultivation areas, the house itself and also the surrounding buildings had to be tackled. With the exception of their first years at Waterperry, when, of necessity, the net had to be cast further afield, pupils were recruited mainly from well-off, upper-class families. Waterperry School of Horticulture was, to some extent, a gardening-style finishing school where young women could usefully bridge the time between leaving school and being presented in society. In line with the school's aim of training 'lady gardeners', the young women were expected to wear a uniform. This consisted of brown knee breeches, a coordinated overall and thick woollen stockings, plus a brown felt hat for outings or the morning visit to church. Although the knee breeches were replaced by overalls after the Second World War, the distinctive and thoroughly practical uniform did not change.

WEEKEND FINERY

At weekends, the atmosphere at Waterperry was probably close to that of a well-run country house. Pupils and staff alike, including Beatrix Havergal, dressed for dinner every Saturday in long evening gowns. However, the horticultural training remained paramount, even if it involved heavy, physical work and spartan living conditions. Despite her rather strict appearance, Beatrix Havergal was a gifted and hands-on teacher who managed to motivate and inspire her pupils. She offered a training course that covered the theoretical as well as practical aspects of gardening. The 1937 school brochure outlined the establishment's goals and curriculum, and provides an insight into the school's guiding principles. The intention was not only to turn out first-class lady gardeners but also to equip them with the ability to lead a team of staff. The brochure pointed out that constructing and maintaining a small garden requires as much skill and knowledge as a large garden created generations ago. A Waterperry training enabled girls to enter the gardening profession whether as part-time gardeners, market gardeners or landscape gardeners.

ALL-ROUND EDUCATION

In addition to the vocational studies it offered, the school also fostered other interests since Beatrix Havergal, who was herself musically gifted, believed that an educated girl should be capable of a good deal more than gardening – she strove for an all-round education, something which even now is often neglected. Waterperry students had the advantage of being close to the University of Oxford, where they could pursue their intellectual and artistic interests. Moments of free time at Waterperry were often spent in an idyllic way, enjoying picnics in the meadows or bathing in the river.

The curriculum was designed to increase the girls' knowledge year by year. The first year taught students the basic skills of gardening; by the end of the second year, they sat a Royal Horticultural Society exam; then in the third year they could specialize in a specific area. Guest speakers helped provide the girls with a comprehensive knowledge of plants and design. Students were also encouraged to develop a nose for business, to which end they were expected each week to sell Waterperry produce from a stall in Oxford's indoor market. The school even exhibited at Chelsea Flower Show in London. To this day, people enthuse

The island beds at Waterperry were created in 1964 by Miss Havergal from plans devised by Alan Bloom. Asters, ornamental grasses and trees blend to form a well-balanced picture.

about the strawberries cultivated in the glasshouses under the direction of former pupil Joan Stokes and which, over a period of sixteen years, won fifteen Chelsea gold medals.

WATERPERRY'S INFLUENCE

Of all the gardening schools for women, Waterperry probably had the greatest and most lasting influence on English gardens. During the forty-four years from the time it was established until it was taken over in 1971 by the School of Economic Science, it turned out a large number of professionally qualified lady gardeners who were much in demand and were often quickly snapped up to work in England's great gardens. Two former students, Pamela Schwerdt and Sibylle Kreutzberger, were hired in the 1960s by Vita Sackville-West and played a substantial role in the development of Sissinghurst (see page 24). While still at Waterperry they were already known for their lightness of touch, their outstanding knowledge of plants and their willingness to try out new ideas – such as using tobacco plants to add variety and interest to the staple border mixes. Like another notable student, Valerie Finnis (1924–2006), they made the leap from pupil to teacher and contributed to Waterperry's success by introducing pupils to the wonderful world of gardening. Finnis (the girls were always addressed by their surname) worked at Waterperry for twenty-eight years, developing the alpine garden and documenting school life. Armed with a Rolleiflex camera given to her by Wilhelm Schacht, one of the groundbreaking gardeners at Munich's Botanical Garden and himself a passionate photographer, she recorded the world around her. Valerie Finnis consequently became one of the best-known and widely acclaimed garden photographers in the country. Her portraits of plants and of important figures within the world of gardening are contained in Ursula Buchan's book *Garden People: Valerie Finnis & the Golden Age of Gardening*.

A number of the school's last graduates are still working within their chosen profession, employed in some of England's most important gardens and held in high esteem for their extensive gardening knowledge. Beatrix Havergal died in 1980 but her goals live on as an important legacy to the gardening world. Former student Mary Spiller, who returned to the school in 1962 and is now over eighty years old, continues to work untiringly at Waterperry Gardens, upholding Beatrix Havergal's working methods and philosophy.

VISITING TODAY

Waterperry Gardens do not figure among England's most famous gardens, even though they are informative, beautiful and varied, and well worth a visit. The walled garden has been converted into an extremely well-stocked plant centre which sells, as it has always done, a range of plants grown on site. The herbaceous border along the outer edge of the longer wall are still magnificent and a fitting focal point. The 60-m/200-ft bed was originally divided into smaller sections and allocated to students so they could cultivate their art and skills. Their task was to create a bed in which plants would bloom continuously from spring to autumn – a considerable challenge, as many amateur gardeners will appreciate. It was only during the 1960s that this bed, which is around 3.5m/11ft deep, was unified and redeveloped into a splendid herbaceous border.

It was planted in the classic manner, with a triangular cross-section formed by placing low plants at the front and higher species at the back. Among Waterperry's other outstanding features are its fruit trees. The long avenue of espaliered apples, leading towards an orchard and the open countryside, demonstrates how it is possible to achieve the greatest possible yield of fruit from a small area while still allowing for aesthetics. Comprising over sixty varieties, the apple orchards remain very much a commercial concern and also help reinforce the rural nature of the site.

PLANTING PLANS

Beatrix Havergal was never short of ideas and was always finding ways to showcase the new plants on sale in the plant centre, or planning how to integrate new herbaceous beds into the garden. Because she had so little time to design areas herself, she sought the advice of Alan Bloom, a well-known and much-acclaimed nurseryman. Island beds, which could be admired from all sides, seemed to her the perfect addition to the garden so, following an exchange of correspondence and lengthy discussions, Alan Bloom produced a set of planting plans that were carried out in 1964. The island beds remain to this day an exemplary composition.

The Long Walk, flanked by double mixed borders, crosses the apple avenue and leads towards a group of rectangular beds that contain the stock plants for propagation. Even though not planted to a particular design, the blocks of different species give this area a wonderful rhythm. The nursery beds also form a living catalogue of plants, enabling gardeners and visitors to compare different types of cranesbill (*Geranium*), iris, catmint (*Nepeta*) and many other herbaceous plants. Beyond these open beds in one direction lies the Waterlily Canal, a peaceful, contemplative area graced with a Tanya Russell sculpture

Beatrix Havergal (second from right) and her students, in their distinctive Waterperry uniforms.

of Miranda from Shakespeare's *The Tempest*. In the opposite direction, dense, high, yew hedging conceals one of the newer and most charming parts of the garden. It has only one point of entry and would attract little attention from without were it not for the cascade of wisteria that appears to beckon the visitor. Designed in 1986 by Mary Spiller and Bernard Saunders, this Formal Garden incorporates a knot garden and is bordered by a wisteria arch covered with white and lilac cultivars (*Wisteria floribunda* 'Alba' and *W. floribunda* 'Multijuga'/ syn. 'Macrobotrys'). Another enclosed garden, also surrounded by high hedges, was created in 1991 to replace the old rose beds that dated back to Beatrix Havergal's day. The new Mary Rose Garden is a work in progress, continually being improved and augmented. It contains a wealth of ground-covering roses, shrub and species roses, as well as climbers and ramblers growing up and over beautiful oak pergolas, obelisks and posts.

PLANT COMPOSITION

Even the smaller garden areas, such as the long, semi-shady border by the entrance to the gardens, demonstrate a masterly approach to plant composition. Framed by the overhanging branches of a Judas tree (*Cercis siliquastrum*) and set off by the striking dark hues of a purple-leaved hazel (*Corylus maxima* 'Purpurea'), the beds lining both sides of the path are filled with a wide variety of ground-covering plants. Here foliage and texture are just as important as the floral display.

To have had the opportunity to train in such a place, learn about the full spectrum of garden plants, and even design one's own area, must have been an experience without equal. Full-time gardening courses are no longer offered at Waterperry but the principles on which Beatrix Havergal (supported by the calm yet energetic Avice Sanders) founded the gardens are still alive. Standing on the bridge and looking across to the magnificent herbaceous border, you can understand why students and teachers alike felt so passionate about this place and so enjoyed their time here. The whole site, comprising over 3 hectares/ 7 acres, with an additional 24 hectares/59 acres of agricultural land, was like a vast gardening playground situated in the middle of some of England's most beautiful countryside.

GUIDING PRINCIPLES

❉ Comprehensive theoretical as well as practical training underpinned the Waterperry gardening ethos.

❉ Beatrix Havergal believed that many techniques in fruit growing were also applicable to the ornamental garden. If you were able to prune fruit trees and bushes properly, particularly blackcurrants, then you could equally well cut back ornamental shrubs and roses to ensure optimum flowering.

❉ Spring and autumn are the main seasons for gardening work. Good preparation and thorough clearing of the area before planting are crucial to a garden's success.

❉ Accurately assess an individual's strengths and allocate the work accordingly.

SIGNATURE PLANTS

❉ Lupins such as 'Chandelier', 'The Governor' or 'The Chatelaine'.

❉ Delphiniums such as 'Walton Gemstone', 'Foxhill Nina' or 'Summerfield Oberon'.

❉ Aster novae-angliae 'Andenken an Alma Pötschke' and varieties of Aster novi-belgii such as 'Waterperry' (2nd image from top), 'White Ladies' (3rd image from top) or 'Marie Ballard' (4th image from top).

❉ Varieties of sneezeweed (Helenium) (top image) and mullein (Verbascum).

'A Waterperry training enabled girls to enter the gardening profession whether as part-time gardeners, market gardeners or landscape gardeners.'

MARGERY FISH

(1892–1969)

'WE MADE A GARDEN'

East Lambrook Manor, Margery Fish's cottage garden

If Margery Fish's name had been mentioned in gardening circles forty years ago, no further explanation would have been necessary. Back then, this expert plantswoman would have been familiar even to those not fortunate enough to have visited her garden at East Lambrook Manor in Somerset. Many of the plants she raised could be found in gardens all over England and every garden-loving household would surely have had at least one of her books on a bookshelf or bedside table.

Advice from the pen of plantswoman and author Margery Fish was always highly practical and based on her own experience; as a result, her tips are just as relevant today as they were at the time. Her first book, *We Made a Garden*, published in 1956 (and which was originally to be called *Gardening with Walter*, in reference to her husband), can be devoured in one go. Margery Fish was a hit with the entire gardening public. Women, in particular those who had been involved in creating a garden and had struggled at first hand with all the trials and tribulations, felt in tune with her ideas. They could rely on her as a source of reference for all the essential skills: from composting to watering, building paths, staking plants and, above all, clever ways of bringing a garden under control. Her book *Carefree Gardening* encourages amateur gardeners to adopt a more casual approach rather than view gardening as an inflexible, regimented activity. When Margery Fish wrote this book in the 1960s, she was, in her way, as revolutionary as the Beatles. Gardening books at the time were typically written in pseudoscientific style and instructions had to be followed to the letter. Margery Fish, on the other hand, ignored prevailing trends in gardening and developed a garden purely according to her own taste – and this in spite of being under the constantly watchful eye of Walter.

Walter Fish was behind the decision in 1937 to buy a house in the country. As editor-in-chief of the *Daily Mail* he was all too aware of the precarious political situation in Europe. Margery was Walter's personal secretary and an important figure in London's Fleet Street: before she met her husband, she had already made a name for herself while working under the newspaper magnate Lord Northcliffe. The couple eventually purchased East Lambrook Manor at the end of a three-month search, having initially rejected it as a wreck. However, between their first and second viewings the property, which dates back to the fourteenth century, had undergone various cosmetic improvements: untidy bushes had been removed from the front garden, tiles had replaced the corrugated iron on the roof, and the interior walls had been newly painted. Attracted by the cottage-style character of this fairly modest manor house, and by the relatively large rooms, the couple quickly realized that they had found their ideal home. They began the renovation work and moved in. It was only months later that they faced the problem of what to do with the garden.

The garden was small, overgrown and a far cry from the splendour of the cottage garden as it is today. At the time it was divided into a front garden and two small areas behind the house, which were on a slightly higher level and enclosed by stone walls. There was also a variegated sycamore (*Acer pseudoplatanus* 'Leopoldii') growing here that – apart from the apple trees in the adjacent pasture – was the only tree in the garden. Walls ran through the garden to the outbuildings and had to be either removed or altered by replacing the unattractive coping stones with flat slabs that jutted out less. It was left to Margery to carry out all these tasks, and the foundations of her garden were truly laid when she planted her first rock garden plants in the joints and crevices of these walls.

The 'Barton', a circular area in front of the house, was originally the site of a horse-operated apple press but had long since become a jungle. Once the undergrowth had been cleared, however, Margery and Walter Fish had a far better idea of the potential of the place. They planned a driveway to the Malthouse, which was due to be converted into a garage, and a large area of lawn around the sycamore to create an increased sense of space. Borders were placed along the boundary wall and bit by bit the garden began to take shape. Like many other English women gardeners, Margery Fish was in her late forties when she found herself tackling a garden for the first time. Apart from some childhood notions, she had virtually no experience of gardening and mistakenly assumed that her husband was equally ignorant in such matters. However, to her astonishment, Walter Fish was in fact quite knowledgeable and knew exactly what he did or did not want.

The newest part of the garden is on the site of the old apple orchard. Mike Werkmeister planted the trees but the tapestry of ground-cover plants in the Hellebore Garden was conceived by head gardener Mark Stainer, in keeping with Margery Fish's ethos.

PLANNING THE GARDEN

The garden was to be an extension of the house, a plan that ideally suited East Lambrook Manor since the front door opened directly on to the garden. The priority was to design a garden that was as modest and undemanding as the house. They envisaged a 'cottage garden in fact, with crooked paths and unexpected corners'. Walter had definite ideas regarding the paths: they must be made of gravel, laid on the right kind of foundation and be rolled on a regular basis. Like the paths, the paving around the house had to be kept clear of weeds, with the narrowest of joints to prevent plants getting a foothold. Margery would have loved to leave little cracks and crevices for small plants, as had been possible in the walls, but she dutifully complied with her husband's wishes. Anyone visiting the garden today and comparing it with photographs taken after Walter's death in 1949 will notice that Margery did in the end get her own way in this and various other matters.

Margery's nephew, Henry Boyd-Carpenter, described Walter Fish as a Jekyll-and-Hyde figure. On the one hand he was actively involved, creative and willing to take a gamble; on the other, perfectly capable of destroying one of Margery's treasured and carefully nurtured plants if it failed to look 'healthy'. Afterwards, he would congratulate himself on having tidied up the garden. Margery Fish accepted all this

with a sense of humour and equanimity: 'Often I would go out and find a row of sick-looking plants, laid out like a lot of dead rats. It became something like a game.'

Their views differed considerably on the subject of buying plants. Walter considered that lupins and dahlias were the proper sort of plants for the garden, and not the more delicately flowery and leafy plants that Margery favoured. He also thought that Margery did not look after his preferred plants properly – she watered them too little – so in his opinion there was no point in buying yet more plants. Margery got around this situation by saying that any new plants appearing in the garden were in fact gifts, which it would have been too rude to refuse. Gardening with Walter must have been frustrating but Margery did admit that in the long run she learned a great deal from him, even if it sometimes meant doing the opposite of what he advocated.

East Lambrook Manor Gardens opened to the public for the first time in the 1950s, a few years after Walter's death. Word of Margery's talent had spread and she was being asked to write articles and give talks. The garden and Margery's style of writing brought a breath of fresh air into what had previously been a fairly rigid gardening scene; she reflected neither modern ideas nor Walter's conception of a garden. East Lambrook Manor was, and is, a place for plants,

'Pudding trees', as Margery Fish called them, line a path that looks almost set to vanish under waves of lime-green *Euphorbia hyberna*, lilac *Phuopsis stylosa* and red *Salvia microphylla* var. *microphylla* 'Newby Hall'.

The Silver Garden is a feast for the eyes. Set amid the varied textures of plants such as *Iris pallida* 'Argentea Variegata', *Artemisia absinthium* 'Lambrook Mist' and spiky cardoons (*Cynara cardunculus*) are touches of colour from burgundy *Lysimachia atropurpurea*, pretty pink *Dianthus* 'Lilian' and a profusion of other plants.

whether as ground-cover for shady areas, alpines for tiny crevices in stone walls, or lush stands of perennials for the mixed borders. The garden is not to everyone's taste. For some it is too bitty, overcrowded with flowers and lacking a coherent design; but East Lambrook Manor is after all a cottage garden, and so by definition combines new and old in an orchestrated chaos. There are neither rules nor blueprints for such gardens, since each has a particular flair that depends largely on their surroundings – an aspect that Margery Fish was quick to recognize. The wild flowers entering the garden by chance fascinated her as much as cultivated varieties. Plants such as columbines (*Aquilegia*), lungwort (*Pulmonaria*) and primroses (*Primula*) captured her imagination and she cultivated them in their hundreds. Primroses were a particular favourite, planted in the best spots and treated to the best compost, which Margery Fish was an expert at producing. She realized early on that she would have to enrich the heavy, clay soil if

her darlings were to flourish, so every winter around 4.25 cubic metres/5.5 cubic yards of homemade compost were diligently spread over the 0.4-hectare/1-acre garden. Even though the plants looked as though they were left to themselves, they were only flourishing as a result of good traditional gardening practice.

A PROFUSION OF PLANTS

The garden is a mixture – some might say jumble – of perennials, annuals, biennials, bulbs, tubers, corms, trees, shrubs and roses. Planted in profusion, they provide each other with mutual support and overlap or cascade in a way that naturally forms a harmonious picture. According to Margery, roses should not be planted as an isolated group but teamed with appropriate companion plants, and on this matter she was always open to advice. When Vita Sackville-West visited East Lambrook Manor, Margery mentioned her desire to clothe a pear tree and two apple trees with the blooms of a

This is how a cottage garden should look, with roses framing the windows, tubs around the door, and a riot of self-seeding plants like valerian (*Centranthus*) crowding up to the honey-coloured stone walls.

climber. Initially she was not particularly keen on Vita's suggestion of planting *Rosa longicuspis* but nevertheless, when three roses arrived by post from Sissinghurst the following January, they were, as instructed, simply pressed into the ground by the trees – where in following years they flowered profusely from May until autumn. These roses, along with other clever plant combinations such as *Rosa* 'Iceberg' with *Artemisia absinthium* 'Lambrook Silver' and *Iris* 'Paper Moon', were intended to extend the garden's magnificent show of flowers beyond summer's flourish.

Evergreen ornamental shrubs such as *Garrya elliptica*, *Mahonia aquifolium*, *Osmanthus delavayi*, yews, various types of holly, as well as variegated juniper (*Juniperus chinensis* 'Expansa Variegata') and other conifers, can be found dotted around the garden. They contribute to a mix that is unconventional and yet looks right here. Margery had her own ideas on how planting schemes should look, stating that: 'Very informal planting needs the restraint of clipped conifers and dwarf hedges.' As a result, the planting at East Lambrook Manor is not arranged in drifts or blocks but in small-scale scenarios that serve to highlight favourite plants.

After Margery Fish's death in 1969, the house had a succession of owners and an effort was made to turn East Lambrook Manor into a tourist destination. Despite the additions, the garden has retained its essence for almost fifty years and even today still reflects the spirit of its creator, who gardened in a way that was free from convention and affectation. Under the guidance of current owners Mike and Gail Werkmeister, who took over in August 2008, there is every chance that East Lambrook Manor will regain its position as one of England's most important gardens. Mike possesses certain qualities indispensable for the task: a strong interest in plants, a commitment to intensive and detailed maintenance, and an intuitive feel for what the garden needs. He takes care of the trees, shrubs and climbers, pruning them back into shape and replacing them when necessary. As a trained graphic designer, his artistic sensitivity is invaluable when it comes to seeing the overall picture; and as someone who drives a canary-yellow Morgan, he may have just the right amount of eccentricity to get to grips with the place.

The input required at East Lambrook far exceeds that of any ordinary garden, which is why tribute must be paid to head gardener Mark Stainer. He started work here as a fifteen-year-old and, after thirty-five years, is familiar with every nook and cranny. As well as being a link in the garden's continuity, he is an expert gardener with a special interest in perennials. So when the diseased apple trees near the Ditch had to be felled, he created a marvellous new Hellebore and Geranium Garden in their place.

THEMED AREAS

Compared with other listed gardens, East Lambrook is relatively small but is packed full of plants providing year-round impact. During Margery Fish's tenure the garden developed in an organic way. Different themed areas evolved as time went by and Margery's plant knowledge and confidence expanded. Although the plot is fundamentally rectangular in plan, the perception of its shape and size is blurred by the two central buildings, the Malthouse and Cowhouse. The garden appears to wrap itself around these adjacent buildings, which are far more dominant than the manor house itself, sitting unobtrusively in the furthest corner of the property. The unusual relationship of the buildings led to a sequence of different areas being formed – some large, some small; some raised, some sunken – which, thanks to the basic structure provided by Walter Fish, fit together as a coherent whole.

To the side of the house, just above the large, open area of lawn, is the Terrace Garden, bisected by a path lined with Margery's distinctive 'pudding trees' (*Chamaecyparis lawsoniana* 'Fletcheri'). This path forms one of the few visual axes in the garden but, in the true spirit of a cottage garden,

is not completely straight. Narrower paths hardly wider than a trail dissect the lushly planted areas and lead to the Silver Garden, or further on to the Top Lawn, neither of which are much bigger than a small urban back garden. The White Garden is even smaller, closer in size to a large flower bed; and as Gail Werkmeister suggests, is best viewed from below in order to appreciate its full impact. While horticulture is not her field, Gail enjoys the atmosphere of the garden, appreciates the sumptuous profusion of plants and is gradually learning their names.

The roughly rectangular area forming the Top Lawn is a peaceful spot where the garden's pace slows. Here it is possible to draw breath and stand back to reflect on the riot of impressions. Dominated by a multi-stemmed snowy mespilus (*Amelanchier*), it is also an area that is showing its age. All established gardens need rejuvenating; it is just a question of how and when. Mike has planned for this by planting younger trees and shrubs in anticipation of the future, so that the overall effect is retained. As well as introducing a young snowy mespilus to the Top Lawn, near the house he has planted a Spanish broom (*Spartium junceum*) that he grew from seed and had brought with him from his London garden. Surprisingly, on looking through the list of plants Margery had in the garden, he discovered that a Spanish broom had existed up on the Strip near where the plant sales area is today. This and other 'souvenirs' from his previous garden reinforce the cottage garden ethos of East Lambrook Manor; the little pink *Magnolia stellata*, the peony and rockrose, as well as a columnar box plant brought from Rosemary Verey's garden at Barnsley House (see page 60) and a collection of plant containers including old chimney pots, have all found a natural home here.

When seen from the open, sunny terrace, which manages to look bright and cheerful even on dull days, the area behind the Malthouse appears dark, damp and melancholy. But there are interesting discoveries to be made here once the eyes have adjusted to the shade. The Ditch, a natural stream that only rarely fills with water and is humorously known as 'the lido', is home to a patchwork of plants so diverse that it is hard to

Walter's large expanse of lawn behind the manor house is the only open area in a garden full both of rare treasures and wild flowers typical of Somerset, like the teasel (*Dipsacus sativus*) under this variegated sycamore.

The Ditch, with its striking pollarded willows, contains an astonishing medley of plants. In early spring the whole area is covered with thousands of snowdrops.

believe there really is space for them all. These are the luxuriant leafy plants that Margery so longed for. In the old days, when safety was less of a concern, visitors were allowed to make their way cautiously down the narrow stone steps at the bottom end of the Ditch and tiptoe through the thick tapestry of plants such as yellow skunk cabbage (*Lysichiton americanus*), *Ligularia dentata* and the impressive plate-like leaves of *Darmera peltata* (syn. *Peltiphyllum peltatum*). As elsewhere in the garden, ferns and other plants have populated not only the ground but the walls as well, reinforcing the lushness of the planting. Out of the shade cast by the Malthouse the character of the Ditch changes; it is lighter, the banks wider and the planting seems to spill into the adjoining Hellebore and Geranium Garden. The Ditch is magical at any time of year, whether in February when covered with a mass of snowdrops, or in summer with its show of perennials and the sprouting growth of stumpy pollarded willows, which are a reminder of the Somerset Levels.

This back section of the garden either side of the Ditch has seen the most change since Margery Fish's time. When Andrew Norton took over East Lambrook Manor from Margery Fish's nephew, cars parked at the top of the garden and visitors walked through the apple orchard along a winding path towards the Barton. Their first view was of the lawn, the sycamore and the manor house in the distance. It was charming

but ultimately impractical. After the property was sold in the late 1990s and a reappraisal of the site's logistics undertaken, the plant sales area was relocated to the far side of the Ditch, the visitor entrance was moved opposite the Malthouse and a much-needed car park built in the adjacent paddock.

In the wake of all these changes Mike Werkmeister is taking things slowly. He is committed to the distinctive cottage-style character of the garden – which is precisely why he is the right catalyst for East Lambrook Manor and its marvellous team of gardeners and volunteers. He positively bubbles with enthusiasm and is a worthy successor to Margery Fish, as exemplified by his improvements to one of the garden's less prominent areas. The old garden wall next to the Cowhouse was falling apart so he decided to rebuild it with the help of a local craftsman. Little gaps were left in the coping so that rock plants could establish themselves and, as a finishing touch, they found a small stone trough just the right size to be placed at the end of the wall, in which Mike planted dwarf plants like tiny white carnations and delicate *Geranium sessiliflorum* 'Porters Pass'. By adding to the garden's layers of detail in a manner so in keeping with Margery Fish's legacy, Mike and his team are sustaining the magic of East Lambrook Manor, a special cottage garden in which surprises are to be found around every corner.

GUIDING PRINCIPLES

❋ You can't make a garden in a hurry, particularly one belonging to an old house. House and garden must look as if they had grown up together and the only way to do this is to live in the house, get the feel of it, and then by degrees the idea of the garden will grow.

❋ You mustn't rely on your flowers to make your garden attractive. A good bone structure must come first, with an intelligent use of evergreen plants so that the garden is always clothed, no matter what time of year.

❋ Gardens with walls are easily clothed as there are many climbing plants that are quite happy clambering over other plants.

❋ One way to furnish the carefree garden is to leave some of the self-sown seedlings, which nature distributes so freely.

SIGNATURE PLANTS

❋ Different plants come to the fore depending on the season. Valerian (*Centranthus*), spurge (*Euphorbia*) (both shown 3rd image from top) and *Gladiolus communis* subsp. *byzantinus* appear throughout the garden in early summer.

❋ Margery had an affinity with old-fashioned plants such as *Artemisia absinthium* 'Lambrook Silver' (top image, with a salvia), Jacob's ladders including *Polemonium* 'Lambrook Mauve' (2nd image from top) and rockroses (*Cistus*) (4th image from top), plants she wanted to preserve.

❋ Perennial cultivars bred by Margery Fish and available in East Lambrook Manor's plant centre include:

> *Artemisia absinthium* 'Lambrook Silver'; *Astrantia major* subsp. *involucrata* 'Margery Fish'; *Bergenia* 'Margery Fish'; *Euphorbia characias* subsp. *wulfenii* 'Lambrook Gold'; *Hebe* 'Margery Fish'; *Polemonium* 'Lambrook Mauve' (Jacob's ladder); *Primula* 'Lambrook Mauve'; *Pulmonaria* 'Margery Fish' (lungwort); and *Santolina* 'Lambrook Variety'.

'When plants are allowed to grow naturally they make a harmonious picture and the result is a happy garden, and a happy garden is a peaceful one, with a backbone of plants that go on from year to year.'
Margery Fish

ROSEMARY VEREY

(1918–2001)

BARNSLEY FLAIR

The legacy of Rosemary Verey

Things could have turned out very differently. Barnsley House, situated in Gloucestershire, one of England's most beautiful counties, might have been purchased by a private owner who could well have closed its gates forever. This exceptional garden would then have lived on only in people's memories, in books and in photographs. However, Barnsley House has been lucky; as have we, the garden-visiting public, who can continue to draw inspiration at first hand from Rosemary Verey's masterpiece.

When Rosemary Verey, the creator of this exceptional garden, died in 2001 and her son Charles took the decision to sell Barnsley House, there were considerable fears for the garden's future. Since 1970, when the garden first opened to the public as part of the National Gardens Scheme, it had welcomed a constant stream of visitors. Up until the year 2000 around 25,000 people a year made their way to Barnsley, a small village in the southern part of the Cotswolds near Cirencester. It was on the list of must-see destinations for anyone passionate about gardening or the English countryside. Barnsley was a dream garden and Rosemary Verey an inspiration. Everyone wanted to take a little piece of Barnsley home with them, be it a plant or ideas to try out for themselves. It came to be viewed as the epitome of an English country house garden: elaborate, even lavish, infused with an air of romance, featuring long vistas, exuberant flower displays and leafy corners offering peaceful seclusion.

Two hoteliers from the village bought the property and converted Barnsley House into a boutique hotel that perfectly combined the old and the new. The garden was its focal point; guests could breakfast on the terrace, take a drink beside the temple or simply enjoy a stroll. The vegetable garden supplied produce for the kitchen and was even extended to cater for the demand. But the investment and running costs were enormous, too high for a small enterprise, and in 2009 the property was sold to Calcot Health and Leisure. Since then, head gardener Richard Gatenby, who was hired during Rosemary Verey's lifetime, has been able to look towards the future and develop a maintenance plan – an important step, since this is not the sort of garden that can be left to its own devices. Traditional working methods, organizational skills and extensive plant knowledge are essential.

Barnsley House garden is not to everyone's taste; many find the style a little too fussy and flowery. But it suits Richard, which is just as well considering all the time he devotes to it. He likes the complex, multi-layered style of planting, the preference for interesting and special plants, and the predominantly pastel colour combinations – all characteristics favoured by Rosemary Verey. When he applied for a position at Barnsley fourteen years ago, he was interviewed first by Charles Verey (who took over the house in 1988) before being introduced to Rosemary Verey. After they had discussed all the usual job-related business, their conversation turned to whippets. They discovered that they shared a passion not only for this nimble breed of dog but also for Laurie Lee's novel *Cider with Rosie*, and so Richard was given the job.

ENGLISH EPITOME

Despite changing trends in the garden world, magazine editors still love this photogenic garden. Pictures of the Laburnum Walk, or of the Knot Garden or potager, regularly appear in garden and design publications. Barnsley was the ultimate garden of the 1980s and 1990s and its creator, Rosemary Verey, perfectly fitted the image of an English lady. She had, for me, something of Agatha Christie's Miss Marple about her, an air of belonging to the old school. Born in 1919, she grew up at a time when young women from good families were expected to get married and look after a household. Despite this prevailing expectation, she attended University College London, which was then as it is today a world-class university. There she studied economics and social history, but married in 1939 before graduating. Fame and a career as both a writer of gardening books and garden designer did not come until the 1980s, when Rosemary Verey was already over sixty. And it all began with her garden.

All-seeing, all-knowing, always correctly dressed, courteous, full of energy and extremely self-assertive, Rosemary Verey belonged, like the Queen, to the generation that continued working until an advanced age. People treated her with great deference and even today refer to her respectfully as 'Mrs Verey'. She lived

Mrs Verey believed that a garden should make an impression all year round, offering a succession of overlapping highlights. Under the tunnel of laburnum and wisteria, not yet in bloom, brilliant red 'Apeldoorn' tulips provide a striking show of colour. Alliums in bud promise to carry the display through to summer.

at Barnsley House for nearly fifty years, first in the house itself and later, after the death of her husband in 1984, in a smaller adjoining cottage. It is often not appreciated that her love of gardening developed over time. When her husband, architectural historian David Verey, inherited the seventeenth-century house with its 2 hectares/5 acres of garden in 1958, Rosemary Verey was more interested in horses than plants. A riding accident, coupled with the influence of her husband, was to change this. In 1962 David Verey had a neoclassical temple transported stone by stone from Fairford Park, about 12 kilometres/8 miles away, and erected in the far corner of the Walled Garden. He had a special interest in preserving the country's historical legacy through his work as senior investigator of historic buildings for the Ministry of Housing, particularly since this was an era when large country houses like Fairford were being demolished or were falling into neglect as a consequence of high taxation and crippling death duties. Once the temple was in place, it was decided to construct a pool and

complete the area with iron railings, thus laying the foundation of the outstanding garden that was to follow.

Along the vista from the temple, parallel to the high wall, David Verey planted a lime walk using *Tilia platyphyllos* 'Rubra', which was to be kept clipped in the style of French topiary. It was, however, his wife's idea to continue the walk, extending it with a tunnel of laburnum and wisteria. Five *Laburnum* × *watereri* 'Vossii' and five purple-flowered wisterias were planted either side of the path and supported by bespoke but simple metal arches. This was the beginning of the famous 'Barnsley' successional flowering: as one plant finishes flowering it is followed by the next in an apparently seamless transition. This approach was carried through to the ground cover beneath the arches of the Laburnum Walk, where red tulips are succeeded by a mass of purple alliums.

Barnsley House illustrates how gradual development inspired by both beauty and

A smooth, open lawn provides an important natural break between intimate, delicately planted beds, such as this spring border along the edge of the terrace, and the strict formality of the yew domes and the clipped lime tree avenue in the background.

function can benefit a garden. The long herb garden, a tribute to the Elizabethan age, was created in 1976 when Rosemary Verey wearied of always having to walk to the bottom of the garden for her culinary herbs and decided to plant them in a formal bed near the kitchen door. Her husband suggested consulting historic books such as *The Country Farm* (1616), Gervase Markham's revised translation of a French treatise called *La Maison Rustique*. This inspired her to create a long, narrow bed with low box hedging laid out in a diamond pattern, thus providing separate compartments for each herb. By cleverly combining the useful with the aesthetic, dill, chives, coriander and thyme were elevated to things of beauty. And with this mini knot garden barely 2m/6ft wide, Rosemary Verey succeeded in reviving a design feature from the past.

Being inspired by others is nothing new, as is evident throughout the history of garden design. Regardless of where the ideas come from, however, it is important above all to choose the right design for one's own garden. Slavishly copying other people was not Rosemary Verey's style. Head gardener Richard Gatenby relates how she wrote him this dedication inside one of her books: 'Hope you enjoy having your input.' It is this sentiment that prevails at Barnsley House, seeking inspiration then adapting it to fit one's own vision. As well as drawing on influential books of previous centuries, the Vereys visited nearby gardens, including Hidcote Manor. They both came away impressed but decided that 'while each part of our garden must have its own theme and character, the garden as a whole would not benefit from being divided into such clearly defined "rooms".' The Vereys had made a wise choice, as the garden at Barnsley House is considerably smaller than Hidcote. In addition, the layout of their plot is different, featuring a park-like front garden sloping down to the road and a roughly square main garden at the back. It was for this reason that the Vereys decided against severely trimmed hedges, preferring to use decorative shrubs and herbaceous borders to screen and define separate areas.

The neoclassical temple, rescued from a nearby stately home, was to some extent the linchpin of the new garden. The metal gates open on to a long vista stretching towards the Laburnum Walk.

The flower beds at Barnsley House are deep, in some cases more than 5m/16ft, allowing plenty of room for trees and shrubs as well as perennials and bulbs. It is only by analyzing the beds in detail that the complexity of the plant schemes become apparent. The beds are built up in layers towards the centre where they form a high point, almost like a curtain, filtering the views beyond and thereby creating a sense of depth. All plants are of similar weighting, all equally important, and they merge to form an exquisite yet complex composition reminiscent of a fine Gobelin tapestry. This type of planting became Rosemary Verey's signature style, and although labour-intensive and costly was exported the world over.

In her book *Rosemary Verey's Garden Plans*, she describes her first steps in the design process and how she found it was something she enjoyed doing. She realized that 'the position of the house, the path lined with yew trees and the 1770 stone wall around the garden made it impossible to be too precise. On the ground, so long as you keep a certain symmetry, you do not notice the discrepancies that seem obvious on paper.' The garden is distinguished by a structure that is neither rigid or forced but acknowledges the quirks of its setting. It is also the loose symmetry that balances the garden. Quick to learn, widely read and prepared to listen to suggestions, Rosemary Verey adopted an important piece of advice from the garden designer and plantsman Russell Page: 'Every garden needs an open space for you to walk into, a place where you can take a deep breath, contemplate your surroundings and enjoy the moment.' At Barnsley House, the large lawn behind the house fills this role. It creates a sense of space, being a neutral, calm area separate from the three-dimensionality of the planting. Standing with your back to the house, you can sense that the garden extends outwards at either side. Parallel to the Laburnum Walk and contrasting with its formal feel is a set of beds planted in a more country garden style. Gold and green are the predominant colours here, provided by Bowles's golden grass (*Milium effusum*

Paving, plants and colour: three elements of the iconic Laburnum Walk. It has been copied many times but nowhere else is the effect as perfect as at Barnsley House.

'Aureum'), hostas, lamium and many others, the names of which would fill several pages.

When appropriate, Rosemary Verey kept things simple and functional. Before making the herb garden, she planted a knot garden beside the house so it could be viewed to best advantage from the window of an upstairs room. For the design of the two squares measuring 3 by 3m/10 by 10ft, she borrowed from Gervase Markham's *The Country Farm* and another book, *The Complete Gardener's Practice* (1664) by Stephen Blake. She created the outline of the interlacing knot pattern by using common box hedging (*Buxus sempervirens* 'Suffruticosa'), gold-edged *B. sempervirens* 'Aureovariegata', shrubby germander (*Teucrium × lucidrys*) as well as topiary box balls and *Santolina chamaecyparissus*. The compartments were filled with gravel to emphasize the rhythm of the hedging weaving in and out. Rosemary Verey could be credited with reintroducing knot gardens, which were fashionable during the Renaissance, to the wider gardening public. By the end of the 1980s every garden worth its salt had a knot garden; in London there were even some tiny gardens that consisted of a single love-knot. Word of Barnsley's magic began to spread and Rosemary Verey became sought-after as a garden designer. Although she only designed two gardens in their entirety – those at Barnsley House and a show garden at the Chelsea Flower Show of 1992 – her influence is nevertheless evident in many famous gardens.

People often forget nowadays that Rosemary Verey played a pivotal role in making vegetable gardens chic. Long before it became fashionable to grow vegetables in the garden, Rosemary Verey had designed her own potager, inspired by another Gervase Markham book, *The English Housewife* (1631). However, she did have to wait until 1979 before she could put her ideas into practice, as the incumbent gardener, Arthur Turner, was very set in his ways. The potager was separate from the main garden, lying on the other side of a lane outside the garden wall. Enclosed within its own dry-stone wall, it resembled a miniature version of the famous potager at the Château de Villandry in central France, but in Verey style. Serious vegetable growers might

have shaken their heads at the sight of box-edged beds and colourful arrangements of green and red oak leaf lettuce, but Mrs Verey thought they were splendid and her kitchen garden provided enough fruit and vegetables for the family table. She started a vegetable trend that spread widely, into Europe and other parts of the world. When Richard Gatenby first came to Barnsley House he worked initially in the potager. Yorkshire born and bred, with a father who grew award-winning vegetables, he remembers how he pulled out all the stops to produce some magnificent specimens. Charles Verey, however, declared them to be vulgar. It was, after all, not about competing in the annual village show but all about appearance and elegance. Nowadays this area is tended with great sensitivity by Ed Alderman.

ROYAL INFLUENCE

During Rosemary Verey's lifetime, visitors entered the garden by a route that took them past the glasshouses rather than through the front garden, which did not really feature in the garden visit. The emphasis was on the main garden, on vistas and axes like the yew-bordered path leading up to the house, dotted with thyme and other plants contentedly growing in the gaps between paving stones. Delicate little pink and blue flowers sprang up everywhere so you had to be careful where you trod, but the scent that wafted up from them was deliciously suggestive of the Mediterranean. Prince Charles was so taken with this planting feature that he introduced it, in a slightly different form, as a Thyme Walk in his garden at Highgrove.

As a mark of the high acclaim Rosemary Verey enjoyed in the gardening world, she was invited in 1992 to create a garden for the Chelsea Flower Show. This was followed by further honours: in 1996 she was awarded an OBE by Queen Elizabeth II, and in 2000 featured in the National Portrait Gallery's exhibition *Five Centuries of Women and Gardens*. Rosemary Verey also broke into the North American market, where her style became hugely popular, fulfilling, as it did, all the criteria required of an English garden. It was in the USA that she gave her last public lectures. The links with north America are still intact. All Mrs Verey's garden plans are held in the archives of the New

Inspired by the potagers of France, Rosemary Verey developed a distinctly English style of kitchen garden. Aquilegia, forget-me-nots (*Myosotis*), Welsh poppies (*Meconopsis cambrica*) and topiary form a decorative edging around the vegetable beds.

If one plant combination reflects Mrs Verey's distinctive style more than any other, it is surely tulips (as in 'Blue Diamond', pictured here) underplanted with forget-me-nots (*Myosotis*) and set against a backdrop of neon-green *Smyrnium perfoliatum*.

York Botanical Garden, and in 2012 a biography by American lawyer Barbara Paul Robinson was published, entitled *Rosemary Verey: The Life and Lessons of a Legendary Gardener*. Robinson had the privilege of spending a few months working with Rosemary Verey, thus gaining valuable insights into her career and creative world.

The garden at Barnsley House has inevitably changed in some ways, but has lost none of its distinctive flair. A new generation is learning to appreciate the ambience of the place. These are the city-dwellers who spend their weekends in the country. They are able to enjoy the interiors of this elegant country house hotel, savour delicious food conjured up by the chefs from kitchen garden produce, and wander at leisure in the gardens. Whether they realize it or not, they are caught up in the garden's magic – and one day they may find themselves planting forget-me-nots and pink tulips.

GUIDING PRINCIPLES

❀ Gather and adapt ideas.

❀ Combine a formal framework with lavish planting.

❀ Introduce main axes and vistas, and furnish them with displays of flowering plants.

❀ Build up layers of trees and shrubs, herbaceous plants, ornamental grasses, bulbs and corms.

❀ Integrate historic features in appropriate spots.

❀ Know, appreciate and take care of your plants.

❀ Do not stint on time or money. This type of garden is the very opposite of thrifty and low-maintenance.

SIGNATURE PLANTS

❀ Old-English plants, such as forget-me-not (*Myosotis*).

❀ Honesty (*Lunaria annua*).

❀ Tulips in a range of varieties, such as 'China Pink' (4th image from top).

❀ *Geranium* 'Johnson's Blue' and other cranesbills.

❀ *Lamium maculatum* (spotted deadnettle) or its cultivar 'Pink Pewter' (top).

❀ Bronze fennel (*Foeniculum vulgare* 'Purpureum').

❀ *Laburnum* × *watereri* 'Vossii', seen here with *Allium aflatunense* (2nd & 3rd images from top).

'Having read Russell Page's *Education of a Gardener*, I realized that the terrace in front of the house was too narrow. So we made it wider, and at the same time took the opportunity to lay paving to replace the existing gravel, which constantly required weeding. Then we measured the area beyond the terrace and I settled down with pencil and ruler and made shapes to fill the spaces – and found what fun it was doing this.'
Rosemary Verey

BETH CHATTO

THE BETH CHATTO GARDENS

Plant communities and new beginnings

The first thing I was shown was the view from the living-room window. Bands of lilac and green flowing away from the house were interspersed with a series of still ponds and the distinctive verticals of swamp cypresses (*Taxodium distichum*). On the far side of this broad, gentle hollow were pink rhododendrons: 'They were my first attempts... in those days one planted rhododendrons. That was before Andrew taught me.' During our conversation, we spoke a good deal about Andrew, Beth Chatto's husband. It was interesting how she always referred to 'our' garden even though the brown signposts on the way from Colchester proudly point towards the 'Beth Chatto Gardens'.

Luckily on the day I went to visit Beth Chatto my appointment was early and the garden was almost deserted, so it was possible to step back in time for a few minutes to the days before the garden was welcoming thousands of visitors. A sense of calm lay over the generously proportioned garden with its ponds, lawns and tall trees. From the living-room window, looking at the garden from a perspective normally enjoyed by Beth Chatto alone, it was apparent that there was something interesting to see beneath the trees in the distance – a green tapestry overlaid with the play of light and shadow. It was these 'green tapestries' that provided Beth Chatto with a title for one of her books. And her success as an author has been attracting a stream of visitors to the gardens since the 1970s. For here, on the outskirts of Elmstead Market in Essex, north-east of London, Beth Chatto achieved the impossible: she created a garden where none should have existed

UNIQUE STRENGTH

The Beth Chatto Gardens do not match the general image of an English flower garden. There are very few roses to be seen and no mixed borders in the traditional Jekyll style. The most striking first impressions are of the park-like grounds and the exceptional feeling for plants evident throughout the 6-hectare/15-acre garden, which also includes a plant centre. Within the spectrum of English gardens, Beth Chatto's does not fit into a particular category but has a character all its own. And therein lies its strength. Because the range of different conditions within the garden has given rise to a series of themed areas, the result is an extremely varied garden containing an immense breadth of plants. At the same time, thanks to the way one area flows seamlessly into another, you are not conscious of the garden being divided into sections but can appreciate it as a single entity. The toughest problems any site can present, including boggy ground, standing water, shade and drought, are all to be found somewhere in this garden, either in the Water Gardens, Woodland Garden or Gravel Garden. Although the practice of planting to suit the prevailing conditions has been popular in Germany for decades and is endorsed in the writing of influential nurseryman Karl

Foerster (1874–1970) and pioneer horticultural scientist Richard Hansen (1912–2001), it is to some extent a new concept in England. Beth Chatto's contribution to the English garden scene is therefore considerable: since the 1960s she has based her choice and siting of plants on ecological principles, becoming a pioneer and an inspiration for generations of gardening fans throughout the world.

NEW GROUND

What many visitors tend to forget, or perhaps do not even realize, is that prior to 1960 there was no garden here at all. It came into existence through hard graft. The lower area was uncultivated land unfit for farming, too dry on the slopes and too boggy in the hollows. The upper section, where the car park and Gravel Garden are now located, was part of a fruit farm that Andrew Chatto had inherited. Photographs taken in those early days, now on display in the cafe, bear witness to Beth Chatto's impressive achievements. She is unquestionably one of the most important figures in the gardening world. The last of her generation, she has learned everything from scratch and shares her vast knowledge and expertise with others, yet remains completely without affectation.

The garden was initially intended purely for the Chattos' enjoyment; a private garden planted around a split-level house which optimized the lay of the land and was at the time, in 1960, a cutting edge design by Essex architect Bryan Thomas. The lower section of the white-painted house is open-plan and airy, comprising the living room at the lowest level and the dining room half a level higher, both with windows opening on to different aspects of the garden. The living room not only faces the Water Gardens on the west side but also the Mediterranean Garden and Scree Beds on the south. It was here, looking out at a terrace featuring a spreading *Magnolia* × *soulangeana* and tubs of plants, that I met with Beth Chatto.

'Let us start.' Instead of talking about herself, she began by describing her husband's life. As a young boy in Laguna Beach, California, 'almost a hundred years ago', Andrew Chatto

Shade and boggy ground are among the most challenging conditions a gardener can face. In Beth Chatto's garden there are countless examples to provide hope and inspiration, such as this combination of umbrella plants (*Darmera peltata*) with candelabra primulas and ferns.

Rhododendrons were among the first plants that Beth Chatto chose for her garden. In the course of time they were joined by many other species, such as the delightful Japanese snowball (*Viburnum plicatum* f. *tomentosum* 'Mariesii').

was fascinated by the wild-growing Californian lilac (*Ceanothus*) and bright orange California poppies (*Eschscholzia californica*), and wanted to know how they came to be there because he had previously only seen them growing as cultivated plants in gardens. This interest in ecology was to define his life. After the Second World War he came across an ecology textbook in Russian and taught himself the language – he already had a command of German and French – purely so that he could discover what information it contained. Hiking in the Alps, sometimes with his wife, whom he married in 1943, also helped to extend his knowledge and formed the basis for his subsequent involvement in gardening.

NEIGHBOURING PLANTSMAN

Sir Cedric Morris, a painter and outstanding plantsman, was another major influence on Beth Chatto. He owned the celebrated Benton End garden in Hadleigh, not far from Elmstead Market, and gave the novice gardener all kinds of advice as well as cuttings and plants which formed the initial stock for what is now the perennial nursery. One of his paintings hangs on the living-room wall. The talk of plants and flowers led the conversation round to the subject of yet another influence, the Colchester Flower Club, founded by Pamela Underwood. Flower clubs became popular after the Second World War and could be found in towns and villages throughout England, as Beth Chatto explains: 'At a time when rationing was still in force, this was a creative pastime. Plants were collected from the garden and arranged according to the Japanese golden rule.' This reference to the triangular form represented by earth (below), heaven (above) and man (in front) does much to explain how plants are arranged in the garden, as there is always a foreground, background and height in Beth Chatto's planting. Another consequence of her membership of the flower club was the interest shown in the material she used for her

A sweep of *Lysimachia ciliata* 'Firecracker' partners pink-flowered bistort (*Persicaria bistorta* 'Superba') in dappled shade, their colours vivid against the green background.

arrangements. When asked where the young Beth Chatto had acquired her wonderful hostas and other foliage plants, she replied 'from my garden'. Given her obvious talents, she was sent off to set up flower clubs in other areas and in doing so came into contact with like-minded women interested in plants. As the demand for her foliage plants increased so did her interest in unusual species and cultivars. At the time, however, no one could have guessed that her collection of foliage plants would take her to the Chelsea Flower Show and win her ten gold medals.

ARRANGER'S COMPOSITION

Beth Chatto considers shape to be as important as colour, and the triangular composition drawn from flower arranging as 'a means of drawing the gaze upward'. She also likes the 'controlled calm of a manicured lawn', like the one extending the length of the garden. Texture and foliage stand out exceptionally well against

a foreground of mown grass; and the lawn also helps to link together the garden's different areas. With over sixty years of gardening expertise, fifty of these in Elmstead Market, any conversation with Beth Chatto is bound to be rich in wise advice – as are her many books. She regards her garden as 'a teaching garden, a place to help solve difficult problems, for example if an area is too wet, too dry or too shady.'

Of course, she did not get everything right first time around, but plants had a better chance of success because she stuck to ecological principles. She was always guided by the location and existing soil when choosing what to grow where. Compost as well as bark and straw mulches are vital ingredients in the garden; the former enriches the soil, while mulching retains moisture and discourages weeds.

The Woodland Garden at the far end of the property is a place of perfect harmony. A little

In the Mediterranean Garden by the main house, a skilful selection of ground-cover plants luxuriates beneath a Judas tree (*Cercis siliquastrum*).

stream runs through the middle and the ground is covered with lush plants in every tint of green, exemplifying Beth Chatto's masterly use of shade-loving plants. Royal ferns (*Osmunda regalis*), variegated butterbur (*Petasites*) and paperbark maple (*Acer griseum*) with its striking, reddish-brown trunks, conjure up a restful oasis. For Mim Burkett, an Australian visitor whom I met during my tour of the garden and who, like me, could scarcely tear herself away, this garden was a must-see. During the devastating bush fires in 2009 she had lost everything – house, garden, nursery and the precious collection of Beth Chatto books that had so inspired her to make her first garden. And it was Beth Chatto's example that helped her tackle the seemingly impossible task of rebuilding her garden and starting Yellow

House Heritage Perennials again: 'There are people in your life whom you want to thank and Beth Chatto is one of these.' There must be lots of people who share this sentiment, whether in Cornwall, Lincolnshire (see page 106) or Ireland (see page 162). Beth Chatto has given amateur gardeners everywhere the motivation to cope with difficult situations.

CROWNING GLORY

The crowning glory of her achievements is the Gravel Garden. Sumptuous, packed with a profusion of flowers, with fluid contours and exciting compositions, this is an outstanding example of planting for our times. It was constructed in 1991 on a site where virtually nothing could thrive. The soil was not only dry, poor and gravelly but also compacted,

The diversity of plants in the garden is simply astonishing. Pictured here are velvety, tall bearded 'Black Swan' irises surrounded by spurge (*Euphorbia*), mullein (*Verbascum*) and *Allium hollandicum* 'Purple Sensation'.

having previously been used as a car park. Even though surrounded by a high hedge, it was also extremely windy. That any plants at all could thrive here seemed unlikely – a real challenge for Beth Chatto. The way she has managed to transform this barren, inhospitable area into a garden is truly impressive. Silvery-green grasses punctuate the beds, mulleins (*Verbascum*) have self-seeded, trees such as Pride of India (*Koelreuteria paniculata*) flourish in partnership with tiny, drought-loving, red *Tulipa hageri* and graceful pasqueflowers (*Pulsatilla vulgaris*). The planting is amazingly lavish and colourful considering that this is one of the driest regions in England. There is strictly no watering in this dry garden – no hidden irrigation systems – for in Essex hosepipe bans are frequently in force. These are simply the right plants in the right place, forming a sustainable community of great beauty.

BEYOND FASHION

The garden is not governed by fashion but has found a style of its own. In fact, Beth Chatto is wary of certain trends: 'Many species plants, such as *Astrantia* and *Heuchera*, have become popular and it pains me to think that these plants are being treated like bedding.' She compares the garden to a theatre showing plants that are best suited to particular conditions. The Scree Beds, constructed in 1999 partially on the site of the Mediterranean Garden, are a good example of this philosophy and in many ways constitute the finishing touch to an extraordinary garden. They were created for smaller alpine species that would have been smothered in

This small, private courtyard next to the house is a place where Beth Chatto can still garden and observe her favourite plants despite her advancing age.

the Gravel Garden. As fate would have it, when Andrew Chatto, who had a special fondness for alpine meadows, died in 1999, this garden was his last view of the world. His research work, fundamental for the development of the gardens, has since been meticulously transcribed from the original notes by a team of typists under the guidance of Noël Kingsbury, garden designer and advocate of naturalistic planting. In laying the foundation on which his wife built, Andrew Chatto made a major contribution to the art of gardening.

TIMELESS QUALITIES

Nowadays, four gardeners are employed to take care of the garden and other members of staff are employed in the plant centre, which has become one of the most acclaimed herbaceous nurseries in England. Beth Chatto no longer spends quite as much time outdoors. With her slim build and direct gaze, she has the gift of expressing her thoughts with enviable clarity. She does not look anything like her age (she was born in 1923) and like her garden possesses a certain timeless quality. Her passion for plants

is based on common sense, observation and years of accumulated knowledge. As she herself acknowledges, she had the good fortune of being a housewife during her younger years and was able to look after the home, children and garden – an arrangement that is no longer possible for the majority of young women today.

In 2001 she was awarded an OBE. In 2008 an exhibition of her work was held in the Garden Museum in London, and in 2010 the Beth Chatto Gardens celebrated their fiftieth anniversary. Despite all the awards and accolades, she still has both feet firmly on the ground – as you might expect from someone who is a gardener through and through. A young boy visiting with his parents was asked by Beth Chatto whether he enjoyed being in the garden. 'Yes, I do,' he answered, 'but it's hard work.' 'Do you like playing cricket?' replied Beth Chatto. 'If you enjoy doing something, you don't mind the hard work.'

GUIDING PRINCIPLES

❋ 'Making a garden is like making a family, the urge to create and nurture is what drives us on year after year.'

❋ 'Be guided by nature: plant the right plants in the right place.'

❋ 'Editing is important in a garden – some plants have to be removed, including weeds. These are simply plants which one does not want in a particular place.'

❋ 'Plant in such a way that the gardener's hand is not in evidence and the plants 1) look at home and 2) are able to develop.'

❋ 'It is very rewarding to make a mistake and then recognize why it happened.'

SIGNATURE PLANTS

❋ Wormwood (*Artemisia*) 'acts like a full stop at the end of a sentence'.

❋ *Bergenia cordifolia* – 'for its flowers and for its leaves'.

❋ Foam flower (*Tiarella cordifolia*).

❋ Barrenwort (*Epimedium*).

❋ Balkan cranesbill (*Geranium macrorrhizum*).

❋ Bugle (*Ajuga reptans*).

PLANT PORTRAITS

From the garden (from top to bottom):

❋ *Nectaroscordum siculum* in front of a cascade of Spanish gorse (*Genista hispanica*) in the Gravel Garden.

❋ White foxglove with Bowles's golden grass (*Milium effusum* 'Aureum'), also in the Gravel Garden.

❋ *Weigela florida* 'Foliis Purpureis' in the Woodland Garden, with ferns and hostas.

❋ Showy candelabra primulas at the water's edge.

'I see my garden as a teaching garden, a place to help solve difficult problems, for example if an area is too wet, too dry or too shady.'
Beth Chatto

MARY KEEN

MARY KEEN'S PRIVATE REFUGE

Vistas, visions and possibilities

'Do not describe me as an English flower lady,' urged Mary Keen when I talked to her about appearing in this book. The thought had never crossed my mind that this energetic woman, who has made a name for herself as a columnist and garden designer, who ignores fads and fashions and takes a subjective approach to gardens, could ever be confused with the type of lady who wanders through her garden with a trug of flowers on her arm. Although from an aristocratic family and as the daughter of the 6th Earl Howe entitled to be addressed as Lady Mary Keen, she comes across as free of affectation and is an expert in the art of understatement.

Well-read, rather intellectual, with an exceptional talent for design and a gift for the written word, she is one of the most celebrated figures of the English garden scene. She is also one of the few people assured enough to speak out on sensitive issues such as the tragic end of Hadspen Garden or the shortage of professional gardeners.

Mary Keen is at the peak of her gardening career, designing sophisticated gardens for famous clients. She was assisted on many recent projects by Pip Morrison, a young, talented landscape architect who trained at Edinburgh University and gained his practical experience under Christopher Lloyd at Great Dixter. Like many of the women gardeners in this book, Mary Keen found her way into the gardening world quite by chance. While her friends were still living in flats in London, she was already a young mother with responsibilities. As well as looking after the home and children, she was keen to find additional interests and was encouraged by her mother-in-law to take on the garden. Herself a talented painter and gardener, the senior Mrs Keen gave Mary such a thorough initiation into the mysteries of gardening that after just a few years her friends began asking for design advice. It was by this route that she became a garden design consultant. Books and articles followed, and Mary Keen soon found herself moving in distinguished gardening circles.

It would be quite wrong to think that her design and journalistic commitments – including columns in the Saturday edition of *The Daily Telegraph* and the Royal Horticultural Society's monthly magazine *The Garden* – leave her no time to attend to her own garden. Located just north of Cirencester, in Gloucestershire, her garden is a private refuge rather than a show garden; a place specifically created for her own needs and those of her family. The Old Rectory at Duntisbourne Rouse (not easy to find without detailed directions) is hidden away within a labyrinth of narrow, winding country lanes. Time appears to have stood still deep in this ancient piece of English countryside. The fields here are smaller than elsewhere, deciduous woodland crowns the tops of rolling hills, and the whole area is steeped in a soothing sense of peace. Such spots are rare: to develop a garden in harmony with these surroundings is a challenging prospect.

SHADED LANDSCAPE

When the family moved here in 1993, the garden consisted of an area of lawn in front of the house, an odd sort of heather garden and an azure-blue swimming pool, all set in deep shade. The surrounding fields, woodland and gently undulating topography were invisible from within the 0.8-hectare/2-acre garden, which might just as well have been in a city suburb as set in the midst of such a bucolic landscape. What was lacking was a sense of atmosphere, and romance. Had this been a commission for a client, Mary Keen would have proceeded quite differently. However, the Old Rectory is her own garden and she makes clear that her personal criteria are different. She wanted it to be a place for the family to feel comfortable in and retreat to. It was to draw in the surrounding landscape yet also provide secluded areas. A kitchen garden was needed but not one so labour-intensive as to require several gardeners. And above all, the garden's overall design should be such that the

Flowers play a
subordinate role in
the garden compared
to shape, which is
used to create superb
effects. This scenario
(opposite) composed
of the simplest of
elements makes
masterful use of
light and shade.

Pillars of the box variety *Buxus sempervirens* 'Greenpeace' surround a large copper pot in the Summer Garden. The pot is planted, like the flower beds, with scarlet, pink and purple tulips such as *Tulipa* 'Queen of Night' and *T.* 'Couleur Cardinal'.

Keens could manage it alongside their other commitments, with only occasional help.

OVERALL PICTURE

Mary Keen considers a garden's ambience to be a vital consideration. Rather than focusing on individual plants, she is always looking at the overall picture, creating focal points and opening up vistas which reflect the spirit of a place. She favours an informal formality in which boundaries are blurred, and while nature has a place in the garden it should never dominate. Above all, Mary Keen seeks to highlight the possibilities of a place. In the case of the Old Rectory, all the essential components were present but they lacked a cohesive framework that would show them off to their best advantage. The picturesque church of St Michael's, its interior adorned with medieval murals, stood forlorn in the middle of the adjoining field, and like the quaint outbuildings by the main house and the landscape itself, was positively crying out to be incorporated into the garden. Appreciating that a formal design would

have been out of place, Mary sought a more subtle solution, an invisible framework that would pull everything together. In addition, the garden was not to consist solely of a series of highlights but also include tranquil, contemplative corners echoing the atmosphere of the place.

Knowing that first impressions are paramount, Mary Keen insists that visitors enter her garden by a particular route. If she herself is not there to welcome the party at the entrance to the drive, the instructions are to follow the gently sloping shaded drive up to the bend, then fork off following the narrow path between trees and shrubs until the vista opens up and you are standing at the end of a generous rectangular lawn with a view of the house. Flanked by vegetation on either side, this open area has a spacious and reflective quality and is a wonderful introduction to the garden. Just looking at the tall, two-storey former rectory with its doll's-house facade gives you the sense of stepping into a period drama. Mary is quick to point out

The juxtaposition of geometric shapes and informal groups of flowers, as shown here around the porch, is evident throughout this highly personal garden, designed by Mary Keen as a place for family members to enjoy.

that the facade has no great architectural merit, but with plant pots arranged around the front porch and roses draped over the stone walls it does have great charm. Yet there is no clue as to what the rest of the garden will be like. Driven on by curiosity, you soon discover that this is a garden which opens up gradually, constructed on different levels so that it is impossible to predict what is around the next corner.

Since there is no hierarchical organization in the structure of the paths, no separation into main and side paths, the choice of where to wander once the visitor reaches the front of the house is left open. Should I turn left towards the yew pillars, which are just visible, or right, towards the gap in the hedge? Individuals with a more adventurous spirit opt for the gap in the hedge and are surprised to find themselves looking down on a garden out of which four tall columns of *Buxus sempervirens* 'Greenpeace' rise. This is the Summer Garden, an area that appears to be square in outline but is in fact

more like a quarter circle. The fact that the narrow, cruciform paths virtually disappear in summer in a sea of flowers is intentional as Mary Keen wants people to brush against the plants, feel them at close quarters and be obliged to stop and look at them. As is the case in the rest of the garden, the overall effect is important. Mary's garden is not designed for a flighty, quick visit or to stroll side by side with a friend, chatting – the paths are too narrow for this – but to school the eye and awaken the senses to the spirit of the place.

SOPHISTICATED PLANTING

In the Summer Garden, colours and shapes capture the attention. A framework of shrubs, chosen for their form and foliage, both serves as background and provides highlights, living evidence of Mary Keen's extensive plant knowledge: silver buckthorn (*Rhamnus alaternus* 'Argenteovariegata'), *Magnolia* × *soulangeana* 'Lennei' and *Buddleja davidii* 'Dartmoor', as well as roses including *Rosa* 'La Reine Victoria',

R. 'Constance Spry' and R. 'Mme Isaac Pereire'. Pink, scarlet and purple are the predominant tones. Once the tulips have finished flowering, it is the turn of perennial honesty (*Lunaria rediviva*), comfrey (*Symphytum × uplandicum*), as well as peonies, irises and giant thistle-like *Onopordum*. The planting appears anarchic; it is not arranged according to height but interspersed with tall perennials rising up at frequent intervals. What Mary Keen has achieved is to develop and freshen the cottage-garden look and make it her own. The planting bears testimony to her masterly expertise and her passion for the unusual, such as the almost purple-coloured honesty (*Lunaria annua*) collected in Corfu and now flourishing in this sheltered, sunny spot.

The excitement of the Summer Garden is followed by calm; an opening in the hedge leads to the Pool Garden and brings a change of mood. Enclosed by yew hedging, the rectangular swimming pool is surrounded by lawn, creating an area which could not be simpler. Following on from this is another opening where formality gives way to more natural surroundings, described by Mary Keen as 'the dell, a wild place with species *Malus*, *Crataegus* and *Euonymus*, and roses, and surrounded by banks of snowdrops which are followed by blue *Anemone blanda* and *Anemone apennina*.' From here a long, narrow path guides the visitor along the boundary to two strategically placed yews, which frame a view of the church.

EXUBERANT COLOURS

The path then takes the visitor with great finesse up a slight slope to a small apple orchard, passing the schoolhouse and the hellebore borders en route to the 'loud beds' either side of the gate leading into the Kitchen Garden. Whereas white flowers were banished by Mary from the Summer Garden, they are on full show in this area. No attempt has been made to stick to a specific colour scheme: the gaily coloured and casual profusion of plants includes old-fashioned light brown and pale yellow bearded irises – Mary Keen finds the modern cultivars 'too frilly' – along with blue aquilegias and the lacy white flowers of umbellifers. The result is

glorious and refreshing. Compared with this kaleidoscope of colours, the meadow under the apple trees on the other side of the path appears almost disciplined, even restrained. Having come finally to a halt, you suddenly become aware of the panorama visible from this point in the garden. Looking towards the house and into the landscape beyond, it seems as if the meadows and woods form part of the garden. Punctuated by the yew pillars of the lower terrace and framed by the apple trees in the orchard, this is the epitome of the English country idyll (pictured on pages 10–11). It was this corner of the garden that particularly impressed me on my first visit, the informal structures alongside formal ones, set off by wild ox-eye daisies in the orchard. The more time you spend in the garden, the more you realize how important these contrasts are and how the harmonious sequence of areas is what sets this garden apart.

ENCHANTED PLACE

Another eye-catching feature in the garden is the wooden half-gate leading into the Kitchen Garden. It restricts and frames the view, allowing just a glimpse through into the other side. Entering the Kitchen Garden is like stepping into an enchanted place. In front of you is a magnificent view of the church, beckoning in the distance. Both sides of the broad grassy path are lined with flowers for cutting, such as cornflowers (*Centaurea cyanus*) and sweet Williams (*Dianthus barbatus*), which surround the vegetable beds. Whatever route you choose to explore the Kitchen Garden, you will eventually end up at Mary Keen's long, recently planted 'pictorial meadow mixture' border. Meadows are Mary Keen's latest passion. The flower meadows at the Olympic Park in East London designed by Sarah Price, in collaboration with experts James Hitchmough and Nigel Dunnett from the University of Sheffield, received much acclaim – so much so that 'pictorial meadows' are all the rage and have found their way into many gardens, including Mary Keen's.

Patina, so vital to the feel of an English country garden, cannot be reproduced instantaneously. The knack lies in spotting and making the most of opportunities, as here at the entrance to the Kitchen Garden.

Unlike many amateur gardeners, however, she was aware that annual flower meadows are more demanding and require more maintenance than one might think. After having thoroughly prepared the ground, she scattered the 'pictorial meadow' seed mix developed by the University of Sheffield comprising a wide range of annual species such as *Ammi majus*, *Eschscholzia californica* and *Phacelia tanacetifolia*, and waited to see how they would develop. The first year was marvellous, but to maintain the effect the area had to be weeded and re-sown every year. Mary's solution is ingenious: she added a framework of ornamental grasses such as *Calamagrostis × acutiflora* 'Overdam' and *Deschampsia cespitosa* 'Goldschleier', along with other species including *Chaerophyllum hirsutum* 'Roseum' and *Dianthus carthusianorum*. The hope is that these plants will bulk up and together with the self-seeding annuals be a colourful and airy but easy-to-manage border.

Fittingly, she paraphrases the poet Goethe in saying that a garden does not develop according to a plan but from the heart. Her garden invites you to linger, to sit in one of the niches dotted around the place and to daydream. The longer you spend in the garden of the Old Rectory, the more aware you become of the detail, the subtle alterations that occur as the light changes and as one season gives way to the next. As Mary puts it, 'it is about making the garden accessible – you will see weeds.' She has given her garden a voice, a unique character so natural that the garden could have been like this forever. Like a good piece of music, it is full of rhythm, quiet passages and crescendos, never loud or shrill but well-rounded, harmonious and exciting.

GUIDING PRINCIPLES

❋ As Mary Keen explains in *Creating a Garden* (1996): 'Garden design is much more than just drawing layouts on paper. The process begins by spending long hours outside to build up an intimate knowledge of the site.'

❋ Avoid trying too hard or the result might end up looking contrived.

❋ Incorporate areas to explore and where it feels as if you could lose yourself.

❋ The illusion of an English rural idyll pervades Mary Keen's entire garden, an effect that is not due to flower displays alone but also a carefully conceived framework. The unexpected awaits round every corner.

SIGNATURE PLANTS

Mary Keen would not wish to be without any of the following:

❋ Apple trees (top).

❋ Snowdrops (*Galanthus*), different varieties and species.

❋ Windflowers such as blue *Anemone blanda* (4th image from top).

❋ Auricula primulas, placed on a stand or in a theatre.

❋ Annuals and wallflowers including *Erysimum* 'Bowles's Mauve' (2nd image from top).

❋ Double *Dahlia* 'Arabian Night' and other cultivars (3rd image from top).

'What I want people to see when they come here is not individual plants but the best views and the atmosphere of the whole place.'
Mary Keen

ANNE CHAMBERS

KIFTSGATE COURT

A garden in three acts

Is there a garden enthusiast who has not heard of the Kiftsgate rose? The name in itself conjures up images of romantic, flower-filled gardens bathed in hazy light. If one rose can be singled out as typical of an English garden, then it must be 'Kiftsgate'. But remember, looks can deceive. Those seductive close-ups of delicate, creamy-white blooms do not always do justice to the actual plant. As ramblers go, *Rosa* 'Kiftsgate' is a positive giant. Once established, it will climb and spread its thorny branches in all directions until it forms a dense, almost impenetrable shield over other vegetation just like the rose in *Sleeping Beauty*. It needs room to develop, and regular care – it receives both at Kiftsgate Court.

Kiftsgate Court Gardens are just as much of a surprise as their expansive, vibrant namesake Rosa 'Kiftsgate'. All too often taking second place to its famous neighbour Hidcote Manor, Kiftsgate Court in Gloucestershire deserves a higher ranking among England's most important gardens for it bears testimony to almost a century of passionate dedication. Three generations of forward-looking women – from grandmother to granddaughter – have devoted themselves to the survival and continued development of this exemplary garden. And whereas Hidcote, as a grade I listed historic garden run by the National Trust, has by warrant of its status a certain museum quality about it, Kiftsgate Court as a private garden has a freer rein to combine historical components with newer elements. It thus reflects an enduring fascination with traditional country gardens.

On arrival, there is little hint of the treat awaiting you. The gravel car park to the side of the house is modest, with a collection of plant tables arranged in the far corner by the garden entrance. But perhaps the best indication that there might be an interesting garden here is the lack of a ticket booth – only a small table with a cash box usually attended by Anne or Johnny Chambers, the owners of Kiftsgate Court. This is typical of the personal touch permeating through the garden. A mellow kind of informality prevails, redolent of the English country lifestyle.

PROFUSION OF PLANTS

A narrow path leads the visitor directly into a dense green shrubbery before emerging from the semi-shade into a clearing, where the atmosphere suddenly changes. It becomes lighter, brighter and more exciting; plants, shrubs and trees merge into a pointillist vista in which all conceivable shades of pink are interspersed with splashes of light blue and the occasional white accent. The flowering profusion of roses, campanulas, peonies, lavender, cranesbills (Geranium) and many more, is set against the background of an immaculate lawn with its sharply defined edges. This effortless look, so typical of romantic English country gardens, does not happen by chance; it can only be achieved through an exceptional knowledge of plants and a keen eye for composition. There are no instructions for this kind of planting, just years of practice and experience.

Kiftsgate Court is so much a part of its surroundings that it gives the impression of having occupied this spot for centuries, and the warm, caramel stone of the house forms a fitting backdrop for the fluid, romantic planting. The classical facade and portico are actually Georgian and date from the second half of the eighteenth century, but were moved to this site between 1887 and 1891 when local landowner Sydney Graves Hamilton decided that it was the ideal location for his dream house. He incorporated the Georgian features into his new Victorian manor house and even went to the trouble of constructing a purpose-built railway line to transport the stones from his existing home at Mickleton Manor a few miles away.

PALLADIAN STYLE

The building is reminiscent of the Veneto and the classical villas of Italian architect Andrea Palladio. In contrast to the symmetry of the architecture, the planting appears vibrant and almost anarchic, as if a trace of cottage garden had slipped in and been given a bit of sophistication. The small terrace next to the house is not in the least contrived but informal and quirky, bursting with shrubs and plants which the boxwood edging can scarcely contain. The four square beds, grouped around a central stone column with a sundial, are filled with an enchanting array of flowering plants. Extravagant Paeonia lactiflora 'Bowl of Beauty', a pink peony resembling a miniature tulle skirt, as well as Rosa 'Rita' and R. 'Rosy Cushion', contrast with the walls of the house behind, which are themselves covered with climbers and vines.

When Mr and Mrs J.B. Muir bought Kiftsgate in 1918, it had no real garden. The terrace was paved and the strip of lawn in front of the house gave way to woodland. It was almost a blank

Every part of the spectacular, long mixed border demonstrates how skilfully herbaceous plants, trees and shrubs can be coordinated colour-wise. Here, soft silvery *Stachys byzantina* nestles up to pale pink *Dictamnus albus* var. *purpureus*, with crimson-purple *Rosa* 'Prince Charles' providing height behind.

The Four Squares: low box hedging can barely contain the profusion of flowers. A key plant here is *Rosa* 'Rita', an old rose variety now scarce in gardens.

canvas, and crying out for some tender loving care. After the devastating events of the First World War, people's interest in gardens began to revive and the Muirs, living as it were on the doorstep of Hidcote Manor, were at the heart of this rekindled passion for gardens. Lawrence Johnston, the owner of Hidcote Manor, had moved to this quiet corner of the northern Cotswolds with his mother in 1907. By 1918 large sections of his garden were already completed, so it was natural enough for Johnston, as a neighbour and friend, to provide the Muirs with suggestions and even encouragement when the young couple started developing their own garden in 1920.

INFORMAL DESIGN

Whereas the Hidcote gardens have a strictly defined structure of garden rooms, which lend a sense of intimacy to the large, basically rectangular site, the garden at Kiftsgate Court is considerably smaller and arranged on different

heights over what is essentially a long, narrow plot. As a consequence, the design is far more informal. The paths, beds and plants here are beautifully in proportion to the size and shape of the garden. There is no question of using loud features to draw attention. Instead, all elements contribute towards creating a feminine, sensual atmosphere. In order to put this garden into context, it is important to bear in mind the predominant style of the early twentieth century. Gertrude Jekyll was then at her peak and her gardens had become a status symbol. They were based on a framework of geometric shapes and structural elements such as stone pillars, pergolas and retaining walls, all clad and covered with vegetation. The garden at Upton Grey Manor (see page 12) is an outstanding example of this genre. Jekyll's contemporaries Harold Peto (1854–1933) and Thomas Mawson (1861–1933), who were likewise influential figures in garden design, both integrated a large number of architectural elements, ornamental

The Sunken Garden is both feminine and formal. White-flowering shrubs are a repeated element, including *Deutzia monbeigii*, *Carpenteria californica* and white roses.

features and strong vistas into their gardens. What distinguishes Kiftsgate Court from other gardens of this period is that its design did not slavishly copy a certain style but was based entirely on personal preferences, picking up on different elements and ideas and moulding them to create a distinctive garden. Heather Muir's achievements are remarkable considering that with no training as a gardener she not only shaped Kiftsgate over a period of thirty-six years but also established a dynasty of women gardeners.

UPPER GARDEN

Extending over just 3.2 hectares/8 acres, Kiftsgate is one of the smaller examples of England's great gardens. Its shape is anything but ideal, illustrating how something remarkable can be created under challenging conditions. The upper garden beside the house is banana-shaped: long, narrow and curved around the main facade. Apart from the tennis

court, the so-called 'Four Squares' to one side of the house and the Sunken Garden are the only regularly shaped areas. In the early twentieth century, a favourite design element was to subdivide a garden by a central and series of subsidiary axes. Few are used at Kiftsgate, however, and their effect is gentle rather than dramatic, as with the romantic double-sided Wide Border, 60m/200ft long, which lies along the edge of woodland. Roses such as *Rosa* 'Fantin-Latour', *R.* 'Prince Charles' and *R.* 'Ferdinand Pichard' thrive here among different varieties of cranesbill (including *Geranium macrorrhizum*, *G. psilostemon* and *G.* 'Brookside'), campanulas, penstemons and *Salvia sclarea* var. *turkestanica*. Ornamental shrubs, notably *Deutzia*, *Ceanothus*, *Olearia*, *Viburnum* and *Weigela* are also important elements in the scheme, lending height and forming an important transition to the woodland trees. The beds are not planted in a classic triangular formation, with the tallest plants banished to the back and low ones

In keeping with its location on the edge of woodland, the emphasis in the Yellow Border is on the colour and shape of foliage. *Acer shirasawanum* 'Aureum' (syn. *A. japonicum* 'Aureum') and golden *Rosa* 'Graham Thomas' rise above a mass of green.

reserved for the front. High-growing species are frequently found popping up in the middle of the composition. Heather Muir had a gift for pinpointing the underlying conditions in a specific location and choosing precisely the right plant from a rich palette of species and varieties to make her garden special.

SUNKEN GARDEN

The role ornamental shrubs can play in garden design is evident from the Sunken Garden, which is the product of two generations. Originally planned as a white garden by Heather Muir, other colours have gradually crept in over the years. However, the main plants in this north-east facing garden still set the tone – for example *Carpenteria californica*, which resembles a giant cistus, and a *Deutzia* laden with white blossom. When Heather Muir's daughter Diany Binny took over Kiftsgate Court and its garden in 1954, her parents moved into the house next door. This represented the start of a new era. The plant

collections were evaluated and supplemented. An octagonal pool with an ancient fountain in the centre was incorporated into the Sunken Garden in 1972–3 and framed by the existing groups of plants. The paving was invaded by plants, which established themselves between the cracks as if following Vita Sackville-West's maxim of filling the garden to the brim.

WIDE BORDER

While the Sunken Garden is self-contained, other areas in the long, upper section of the garden flow into one another. A straight, paved path acts as a continuation of the Wide Border, leading to the secluded site of the tennis court surrounded by high yew hedging. Parallel to this axis, between and over the vegetation and entwining itself among the trees, grows the original Kiftsgate rose. Acquired in the 1930s from E.A. Bunyard's nursery as a musk rose, it was later identified as a previously unknown form of large *Rosa filipes* and named 'Kiftsgate' by plantsman Graham

Flanked by a double hedge of *Rosa gallica* 'Versicolor', this path runs between the rose beds towards a sculpture. The axis is accentuated by an unusual arch of *Sorbus aria* 'Lutescens' at the far end.

Stuart Thomas. Compared to the proportions of 'Kiftsgate', the roses on either side of the path appear much more restrained. An unusual touch here is the use of *Rosa gallica* 'Versicolor' as an edging for other roses in colours ranging from pink to magenta, with accents of white and yellow. The rose beds lead to an arch of silver-leaved whitebeam (*Sorbus aria* 'Lutescens') framing a sculpture; this stands in front of a hedge that forms an endpoint to the vista. The *Seated Lady* by Simon Verity was commissioned by Diany Binny and is one of two sculptures created especially for this garden in the 1960s.

REFLECTIVE POOL

Were it not for the half-concealed gap in the hedge, it would be easy to walk straight past and miss out on a thrill. Here, on the site of the former tennis court, is one of Kiftsgate Court's surprises, a modern garden in an old setting. Like an abstract painting, it is designed to be viewed from a distance. It was Anne Chambers, Heather Muir's granddaughter, and her husband Johnny who decided to redesign this area. As they reveal in the guide book: 'For some years we had looked for an opportunity to add our own mark to the garden. When the surface of the tennis court became too uneven and our tennis more a game of chance then skill, we decided to design a water garden that reflected our enjoyment of contemporary design and materials.' The resulting peaceful, contemplative scene forms a welcome counterpoint to the lavish profusion of colour in the rest of the garden. The tennis lawn has been replaced by a dark square of water with a wide paved border. Rectangular stepping stones in light-coloured Haddonstone paving – Portland stone would have been too expensive – with rhythmically spaced, narrow joints lead across the water to a square of grass in the middle of the pool. Rising from the water is a row of delicate stainless steel stems, each topped with a bronze philodendron leaf which, from a distance, resemble water lily leaves. Created by the sculptor Simon Allison, the thin steel rods appear to be swaying in the wind and are reflected in the dark, seemingly bottomless pool. This most recent feature of the garden, finished in 2000 and modelled on Geoffrey Jellicoe's water garden at Sutton Place in Surrey, is undoubtedly a great

asset to the garden. Anne Chambers has been responsible for Kiftsgate Court since 1981 and possesses an instinctive feel for the garden. Like her mother and grandmother before her, Anne has never had any formal training in design or horticulture. What she does have, however, is energy, perseverance and a deep affinity with the place. With over thirty years of accumulated experience, she knows what the garden does and does not like.

VIGNETTES

After the dark pool, the garden seems to have no further secrets left to reveal. A long bed, the Yellow Border, enclosed on one side by a high yew hedge and on the other by a waist-high box hedge, leads back to the entrance. The main focus of attention at this point is the diverse and skilful planting, a combination of different shades of green- and yellow-leaved ornamental shrubs, accented by yellow roses and groups of azure-blue delphiniums. Looking across to the woods, however, you become aware of openings like vignettes cut into the bank of trees, revealing why Sydney Graves Hamilton chose this spot for himself. Kiftsgate Court stands on the edge of a plateau that falls abruptly away to the north-west, towards the picturesque Vale of Evesham. Through these 'windows' in the trees, a view unfurls across the fertile valley to the Malvern Hills silhouetted in the distance. Deciduous trees cling to the slope, giving the impression of dense impenetrability, but at the end of the Yellow Border, half hidden and almost looking like an afterthought, are steps leading down the side of the hill. The trees begin to thin out and a group of Monterey pines (*Pinus radiata*), apparently standing sentinel, create a change of atmosphere.

Heather Muir terraced this slope back in the 1930s. She had a summer house built and planted a diverse collection of tender species, which have been augmented by her successors. Giant viper's bugloss (*Echium pininana*), agave, abutilon, *Acacia*

The house appears to be surrounded by a sea of flowers. Kiftsgate's timeless design continues to be nurtured and improved as it was in past generations, creating a distinctive and romantic atmosphere.

dealbata, cistus and *Puya chilensis*, a bromeliad, thrive in this frost-protected area. Surrounded by Monterey pines, you feel transported to a warmer, almost Mediterranean climate. While Heather Muir enjoyed favourable conditions on her own doorstep, Lawrence Johnston, a passionate plant collector, was obliged to resettle his exotics in his garden in Menton on the Côte d'Azur, in southern France. Then, as now, fellow plant enthusiasts frequently swapped plants and seeds; and it would be no surprise at all if some of the specimens from Johnston's Mediterranean paradise had managed to establish themselves on this slope. What makes this particular ensemble so special is the view of the terrace below, where Anne's mother constructed a semi-circular swimming pool in the 1960s. Modern, yet timeless in appearance, the lawn-framed pool merges perfectly with the landscape. The strong bonds between mother and daughter are much in evidence here for what one began, the

other completed. About ten years ago, Anne had the pool painted black, demonstrating that a swimming pool could be aesthetically pleasing in its own right. She is quite happy spending her holidays at home since, as she points out, when looking up the hill towards the house on a balmy summer's evening, with a glass of wine in hand, it is easy to imagine one is in Italy.

Kiftsgate Court Gardens have a powerful feel-good factor. Even though the garden is regularly open to the public, it still has the air of a private garden. The garden attests to the vision, hard work and close bonds between three special women who not only respected the past but also had the confidence to follow new directions. With the help of just two gardeners, Anne is rarely able to play the fine lady. Her hands are proof in themselves of the hours of work she puts in. Such is the importance to her of the legacy she intends passing on to the next generation.

GUIDING PRINCIPLES

❉ It is important to build upon a garden's legacy. The individual styles of each generation are woven into the evolving garden.

❉ Water features and sculptures should be used sparingly and placed wisely. This maxim was introduced by Anne Chambers' mother Diany Binny. Some of the artworks were designed by Simon Verity specifically for locations in the garden (as beneath these pine trees, 2nd image from top).

❉ Weave in elements of surprise to offset the garden's distinctive rural tone.

SIGNATURE PLANTS

❉ Cranbesbill (*Geranium*) species and varieties.

❉ Various hydrangeas.

❉ Mock orange such as *Philadelphus* 'Belle Étoile'.

❉ Roses, especially *Rosa* 'Kiftsgate' (top), *R.* 'Rita' and the distinctive rosa mundi (*R. gallica* 'Versicolor') (3rd image from top).

❉ *Deutzia monbeigii* (4th image from top).

' There is no question of using loud features to draw attention. Instead, all elements contribute toward creating a feminine, sensual atmosphere.'

NEW
DIRECTIONS

GILL RICHARDSON

WHERE THE WIND BLOWS

Gill Richardson's masterpiece
at Manor Farm

If you analyze where the majority of England's exceptional gardens happen to be situated it becomes apparent that they are mainly in the counties. Here, in rural, outlying areas far from major conurbations and outside influences, is also where exciting new gardens are being made. These are gardens that have either been passed on from one generation to the next, or built with singular flair virtually from scratch, as at Manor Farm, Lincolnshire. The common factors linking all these gardens, and characteristic of English gardens in general, is a love of plants and an appreciation of the gardening skills needed to care for them. Gill Richardson is a fine example, as the creator of superb combinations of plants which blend trees, perennials, ornamental grasses and bulbs in a way particular to this garden. Her talents should not be underestimated.

A rustic throne-like seat of oak placed strategically at the end of one of the main paths and inscribed with the word 'Astrantia' is symbolic of the romantic, yet innovative character of this garden, situated in one of England's least visited regions. As a county predominantly agricultural in character, shaped by the vast wetlands of the fens and the east winds blowing off the North Sea, Lincolnshire is rarely considered one of the country's top tourist destinations. The fields are large and given over predominantly to the cultivation of rapeseed, cereals and potatoes, with only an occasional solitary oak tree left standing as a reminder of the old field structure. Many years ago daffodils and tulips from Lincolnshire used to supply the major flower wholesalers, and the show of colour in the fields attracted visitors from all over England. But that was in the past, and although Spalding is still the centre of England's bulb industry, it has long been overtaken by Holland as a bulk producer of bulbs. Nowadays there is little incentive to visit this corner of east England unless you are an admirer of former prime minister Margaret Thatcher, who came from Grantham, a few miles away from Gill Richardson's home at Manor Farm, Keisby. Perseverance, hard work and passion seem to be qualities typical of the women of this region: the transformation of the garden at Manor Farm into a flowering paradise cannot be explained in any other way.

COUNTRY LIFE

The Richardsons are not one of those families who have escaped from the big city in search of an alternative lifestyle. They have been farmers for several decades, are totally familiar with the climate, soil and location, and harbour no illusions about the realities of life in the country. In Lincolnshire it is hard not to raise an eyebrow when people talk about the benign English climate. Conditions on England's east coast are completely different to those

on the milder west coast. The weather here is determined by the North Sea and, as Gill's husband Adrian Richardson remarks, the wind is sometimes so bitter that it feels as if it has blown in straight from Russia. The Pennine Hills forming England's backbone act as a barrier to rain, preventing its spread eastwards. As a consequence, soils are dry and water is often in short supply. Another important factor is the lie of the land. Contrary to the general misconception, however, not all of Lincolnshire is flat. The area around Keisby is characterized by gentle rises and dips. Its natural topography affords some protection against the biting winds, a factor exploited over the centuries as is evident in the picturesque villages of this area, many of which date back to the sixteenth century. Manor Farm, a listed building dating back to 1620 and built from light-coloured sedimentary stone, blends seamlessly into the landscape. Were it not for the numerous farm buildings it would be easy to drive right past the house without noticing it. In addition, there is no sign of a garden. All that is visible is a large area of hardstanding and a collection of plant tubs packed between the back door and the stable.

ENEMIES WITHIN

Gill Richardson has been working on her garden since the 1970s and is well aware that there is a fine line separating success from failure. Enemies lurk round every corner, be they mice, wood pigeons or muntjac deer (a small species of deer which, to Gill Richardson's horror, seem to regard hellebores as a tasty treat). Badgers are also not the harmless creatures portrayed in children's literature; 'Mr Brock' loves nothing more than to dig up gardens in search of food or simply as a nocturnal pastime. What has been achieved here at Manor Farm, despite far from ideal conditions, would (and does) inspire many a gardener, particularly those with problem areas. Quite apart from the constant wind, the soil is of heavy clay. Mulching is an absolute necessity if plants are to flourish here, as are an

extensive knowledge of horticulture and a good deal of patience. Even if it is essentially Gill's garden, the Richardsons work as a team without any additional help. Adrian's contribution is considerable: he mows the lawns, clears ground, and takes care of all the rough work in this 0.4-hectare/1-acre garden.

The original part of the garden, which you see as you approach along the side of the building, looks from a distance like so many farmhouse gardens, tucked away from the hustle and bustle of the farmyard and consisting of a large rectangular lawn behind the house surrounded by flower beds. However, first impressions can be deceptive and the longer you look around the more you see, and the more you become aware that this garden differs from the norm. The borders, set off by the virtually perfect lawn, mown with broad stripes and sharply trimmed edges, are particularly eye-catching. The planting is constructed in

tiered layers and includes a subtle mixture of trees, shrubs and perennials. Interspersed with a variety of bulbs, including crown imperials (*Fritillaria imperialis*) and tulips, the borders are a wonderful mixture of colours and shapes which flow into each other. Beyond the garden the view continues into a landscape of pastures and woodland. The design is so clever that it is hardly apparent that this part of the garden runs parallel to the country lane, which is hidden behind a yew hedge. While the border along this boundary is relatively narrow, its counterpart on the other side of the lawn has much larger proportions. Beneath the old fruit trees Gill Richardson has planted a carpet of ground-cover plants in multiple shades of green. Snowdrops and many of her favourite astrantias thrive here, including *Astrantia major* Gill Richardson Group and other varieties she has bred herself – which is why groups of plant fans, even from abroad, make their way here to visit the garden (open by

The sheer diversity and dynamic quality of the new Gravel Garden is astonishing: in the foreground (from left to right) are *Delphinium requienii*, *Achillea millefolium* 'Lilac Beauty' and *Centranthus lecoqii*.

Scarlet *Lychnis coronaria* 'Blych' pokes its head up between Michaelmas daisies such as *Aster amellus* 'Vanity' and pale lilac *A. pyrenaeus* 'Lutetia'.

On an open area of grass parallel to the gravel beds Adrian has built a pavilion, or as he terms it 'the bandstand'. Sitting surrounded by a screen of *Deschampsia cespitosa* 'Goldtau' and white *Gaura lindheimeri*, it is a wonderful spot to catch the evening sun.

appointment only). A natural, romantic ambience pervades this apparently peripheral area. Striking groups of *Nectaroscordum siculum* have proliferated in the semi-shade of a corkscrew hazel (*Corylus avellana* 'Contorta'). Their closed buds resemble spears, standing out boldly from the masses of white honesty (*Lunaria annua* var. *albiflora*). Delicate branches filter the light and provide dappled shade, lending a further dimension to the garden.

SPRING BLOSSOM

The well-tended lawn provides a natural visual break from this abundance of plants. Standing with your back to the house, you could easily imagine that the garden ends by the spreading *Magnolia* × *soulangeana*, planted thirty years ago. In springtime when this magnificent tree scatters its blossom over the ground, it looks, as

Gill so aptly remarks, 'as if someone is having a wedding'. The magnolia, however, is merely an interlude on the way to an entirely different area, concealed by the outstretched branches and the masterly semi-shaded planting beneath its canopy. And here lies the charm of this garden: it reveals itself gradually. Gill Richardson uses plants like building elements, creating a multifaceted, natural and romantic ambience with year-round impact. Since there is no clearly defined route through this country garden, you can wander as the fancy takes you. Eventually you will reach the furthermost section of the garden, where vegetables used to be grown but since transformed into a herb garden surrounded by yew hedging and spanned by straight paths. This stronger formal element contrasts well with the otherwise informal design of the garden. And it is here, at the end of one of the axes, that Gill

Gill is constantly devising new plant combinations. Here she has partnered foxtail lilies (*Eremurus ×
isabellinus* 'Cleopatra') with pale yellow yarrow (*Achillea*), clary sage (*Salvia sclarea* var. *turkestanica*)
and mother-of-pearl poppies (*Papaver rhoeas* Mother of Pearl Group).

has positioned the throne-like 'Astrantia' seat,
a resting place from where she can see over to
the newest section of her garden – the vibrant
naturalistic flower beds.

However there is so much more to see even
before you reach this section, such as the first-
rate planting along the banks of the stream
marking the boundary with the neighbouring
property. The steep bank is covered with a
variety of moisture- and shade-loving perennials:
common butterbur (*Petasites*), magnificent
hostas, especially *Hosta sieboldiana*, *Ligularia* and
Rodgersia, as well as astrantia and more. As Gill
is quick to point out, the stream is not always a
peaceful brook but can become a rushing torrent
and burst its banks, carrying everything along
with it. Establishing a meaningful planting
is therefore difficult, and sometimes means

starting again after the winter storms and
battling against nettles, but for Gill it is worth it
because the stream is integrated into the garden.

Until ten years ago, the garden ended at the stone
boundary wall which can still be partially seen.
But when the adjacent farmyard was abandoned,
and no one else had a use for it, the land was signed
over to the Richardsons. The only condition
was that the neighbouring house retained right
of access across the property. The ground was
heavily compacted, bare and exposed. Anyone
else would have avoided tackling an area like
this, but Gill Richardson had a plan. On one hand
it offered an opportunity to continue planting
along the stream and to construct a path, even if
it was only a narrow track along its banks. On the
other, and perhaps more importantly, the new
site provided the chance to create a gravel garden.

The bare plot of land acquired from a neighbouring farm has undergone the most dramatic transformation, and it is hard to imagine that tractors and farm equipment once filled this space. The two island beds of the Gravel Garden brim over with perennials, ornamental grasses and bulbs, as if they had always been here.

Beth Chatto and Piet Oudolf are two of Gill Richardson's role models. She is a particular fan of Chatto's gravel garden and given that not only the climatic conditions but also the land's former use have a great deal in common with Chatto's site, she knew that she stood a good chance of success. The result is remarkable, especially in summer and autumn, when the sun-loving plants and ornamental grasses reach upwards, courting attention. Approaching this area from the damp shade of the stream the contrast could not be greater, as once away from the protection of the trees the wind blows relentlessly and it seems incredible that anything could thrive here. But it is also the wind that adds an extra dimension to the planting, without which the *Miscanthus* and tall *Sanguisorba obtusa* would not sway so beautifully. From a distance it is hardly discernible that the Gravel Garden is comprised of two beds. Having paced up and down the area,

Adrian decided on the shape of the island beds and also brought in truckloads of manure. The rest was left up to Gill, who learned through trial and error what would thrive. Crucial elements in her success are her strong sense of colour composition and her natural instinct for planting.

Gill Richardson prefers plants that look after themselves, such as lungwort (*Pulmonaria*) and ornamental grasses. But there are also hidden treasures, such as *Helleborus* 'Anna's Red', casually but cleverly incorporated into the garden, plants that reflect Gill's passion for striking but delicate flowers. She has gradually moved away from shrub roses and prefers to use climbing roses and ramblers, such as *Rosa* 'Rambling Rector' and R. 'Treasure Trove', which weave their way among and over trees. It is the eye for detail and finesse with layering plants that make Manor Farm such a captivating garden.

GUIDING PRINCIPLES

❋ Adapting: choosing the most appropriate plants for the location and existing conditions.
❋ Water: regardless of how dry the conditions get, plants must be able to survive without additional watering.
❋ Time: work gradually, expanding and developing the garden as one's expertise and knowledge grows.
❋ Teamwork: in the same way that Vita Sackville-West and Margery Fish had the support of their husbands in achieving miracles during the last century, Adrian Richardson's contribution to Gill's success has been similarly important.

SIGNATURE PLANTS

❋ A range of snowdrops (*Galanthus*)
❋ Different species and cultivars of hellebore (*Helleborus*)
❋ Astrantia in variety
❋ Ornamental grasses such as *Miscanthus*
❋ Lungwort (*Pulmonaria*).

New cultivars bred by Gill Richardson (from top to bottom):
❋ *Astrantia* 'Burgundy Manor'.
❋ Two new, as yet unnamed *Astrantia* seedlings.
❋ Striking, red *Astrantia major* Gill Richardson Group.

'Gill Richardson uses plants like building elements, creating a multifaceted, natural and romantic ambience with year-round impact. Since there is no clearly defined route through this country garden, you can wander as the fancy takes you.'

HISTORY REDEFINED

Lady Xa Tollemache and the gardens
of Helmingham Hall

'When I was in my twenties I had no idea about gardening.
Roy taught me everything.' We chatted as we walked, Lady
Xa Tollemache pushing a wheelbarrow laden with gardening
tools in front of her, the dogs trotting obediently alongside.
On the other side of the paved courtyard we crossed into the
garden over one of the two drawbridges that are raised every
evening. Sometimes it is better not to research a place too
much in advance of a visit, as the element of surprise is then
so much greater. This was certainly my experience when I
visited Helmingham Hall in Suffolk, a moated house set
among gardens dating back to 1510 and surrounded by 100

hectares/250 acres of hunting grounds and a large estate.

Moated mansions like this are often found in the Loire Valley, where they tend to be feudal and imposing in appearance. Helmingham Hall, on the other hand, home to the Tollemaches since the early sixteenth century, is quite different. Its understated grandeur is perhaps due to the architecture in red brick, the light-coloured stone surrounds of the windows, the octagonal chimneys and ornamented finials, or the dark latticework pattern ornamenting the facade. Even the castellation is a finishing decorative flourish rather than a means of defence. Despite its substantial size and importance in English history, the property exudes a kind of homely charm. And it was here in 1976 that Xa Tollemache began her 'apprenticeship' as a gardener.

Her teacher was Roy Balaam, who had worked in Helmingham's gardens since he was a boy and by the age of twenty-four had been appointed head gardener. Roy had never wanted to be anything other than a gardener and one can only marvel at his passion and expertise. He did such an excellent job of coaching his rather unusual 'apprentice' that Xa now not only develops her own garden with great aplomb but also designs gardens for other people. In 1997 she was invited to design her first garden for the RHS Chelsea Flower Show, sponsored by London's *Evening Standard*. The judges at Chelsea set great store on plant use in those days, and the country-garden style espoused by Rosemary Verey and Penelope Hobhouse was then riding high. Xa Tollemache's gift for planting design ensured that her exhibit won a gold medal. However, it took the lady of the manor twenty-five years of learning through experience in her own garden before she reached this high point in her gardening career. She and her head gardener, a highly accomplished team, are assisted by two additional gardeners, a part-time assistant and occasional volunteers in tending a total of 4 hectares/10 acres. Low-maintenance is not a label that could be applied to Helmingham gardens. With its magnificent borders, its box and yew hedges, topiary, roses, meadows and vegetable beds, Helmingham encapsulates the essence of a historic country house garden – one not stiff or formal, but with

personality and full of ideas that could easily be transferred to much smaller gardens.

What distinguishes Helmingham is the unusual division of the garden into two distinct sections located on opposite sides of the hall, the larger of the two being on its own island and surrounded by a wall. Seen from above, they could be construed as separate entities; and yet the garden does not feel fragmented, for the hall itself acts as an anchor, as does the moat, and there is a unifying style that borrows elements from Renaissance gardens. The moat is no paltry ditch but an impressively wide sheet of water enclosing the hall on all sides. It acts as a calming, neutral barrier between the building and gardens. The surrounding deer park, a tranquil rolling landscape punctuated by great oak trees, also affects one's perception of the garden. Unusually, the park comes right up to the edge of the moat and occupies the space on either side of the hall that separates the garden's two sections.

SHELTER BELT

As Helmingham is only approximately 20 kilometres/12 miles from the coast, the wind is a constant presence and some form of protective enclosure is essential if anything is to grow. Consequently, the gardens are sheltered behind walls and hedges and are not immediately visible from a distance. By the time Lady Tollemache and I had hurried out from one flank of the hall, across the internal courtyard, over the drawbridge and on to the embankment running parallel to the moat, the wind was whistling around our ears. We were out in the open, surrounded by distant views, following a path mown through tall meadow grass rich in wild flowers, which swept around topiary yew cones and down the steep banks of the moat. An interesting detail was the edge of the path, not straight but beautifully scalloped. Further on, the path met a second moat and at this point was surrounded on both sides by water. A narrow embankment led us across to a rectangular island enclosed

Surely this is the epitome of an English country garden: an uncontrived profusion of perennials and annuals in a wonderful mixed border, set off by the central grass path and the roses in the background.

by high brick walls, where it was stiller, warmer and more welcoming.

When the walls were built in the mid-eighteenth century, they were set back rather than simply following the outline of the island, allowing space for two arms to extend and form a sort of courtyard facing the hall. It was here, in the 1960s, that Xa's mother-in-law, Lady Dinah Tollemache, created the first purely floral area. At the foot of the walls she planted rose beds filled with Hybrid Musk roses such as yellow *Rosa* 'Buff Beauty' and white R. 'Penelope', which she edged with a border of *Lavandula angustifolia* 'Hidcote'. She also planted a simple, formal parterre of box hedging, adorned with two urns on either side of a central axis visually linking the hall on the other side of the moat with the ornamental gates leading into the island's Walled Garden. When this area was remodelled in 1978, the plan was to replace the parterre bedding with plants that would be attractive throughout the year.

Box cones paired with ground-covering cotton lavender (*Santolina chamaecyparissus*) were the obvious choice, a combination still in place today, with only a token ring of bedding plants around the urns. The Parterre forms a perfect approach to the Walled Garden as well as a thematic link to the Knot Garden on the other side of the house.

DOUBLE BORDERS

Aside from the impressive yet delicate wrought-iron entrance gate, the main feature of the Walled Garden is the cruciform double-sided herbaceous border – which is where Xa Tollemache was heading with her plant-laden wheelbarrow. Roy, the head gardener, was waiting here to unload the flowering tobacco (*Nicotiana alata*) and other annuals, and the two of them set to work on the border. Climbing roses, such as *Rosa* 'Albertine', R. 'Gruss an Teplitz' and R. 'The Garland', trained up metal supports, fringe the back of the border and form a semi-transparent screen through which the rest of the garden can be seen. The

Winged horses guard the gateway into the Walled Garden. *Rosa* 'Félicité Perpétue', *R.* 'Prosperity' and *R.* 'Buff Beauty' were planted by Lady Tollemache's mother-in-law.

exuberant borders have a vibrancy and freshness difficult to capture even in the best photographs. Xa and Roy do not follow a dogmatic planting scheme, but combine the perennials with a slightly different selection of annuals each year. This ability to remix traditional elements, give them a twist, is a theme evident throughout the garden, ensuring there is always something exciting to see.

HISTORIC LAYOUT

History hides under the surface of this garden. Back in the 1980s documents were unearthed that showed how the Walled Garden had originally been laid out in the eighteenth century. They revealed a grid system of eight equal-sized rectangular beds divided by paths, metal-framed tunnels running from side to side across the width of the garden and a border following the perimeter of the wall. This exciting discovery led the Tollemaches to do away with the unattractive large squares that had come to fill the garden

and in 1986 reintroduce the historic layout. Fruit and vegetables are grown here, as in the past, but there is a limit to how much the household can consume so ever more flowers are creeping in.

The narrow border at the base of the walls is divided into sections where Xa Tollemache has themed beds such as the potager, where a range of vegetables are grown in an ornamental manner. In the topiary bed, bearded irises left over from one of her Chelsea Flower Show gardens rub shoulders with some amusing box figures: 'the only rabbits in the garden are the topiary ones,' says Xa. She can 'play around' in these beds and try out different colour schemes, like in the small section filled with the punchy colours of what she calls 'firecracker tulips', in bright red, orange and yellow with a dash of purple. Between this bed and its quieter, predominately pastel-coloured neighbour, is a thick slab of yew hedging, a device that Xa has used to great effect in a number of places along the border.

Inside the Walled Garden, the border along the perimeter of the brick walls has been divided by blocks of yew hedging into separate areas each displaying a different theme. This arrangement makes it possible to try out new plant combinations.

FORWARD PLANNING

The mixture of old and new, the combination of ornamental and kitchen garden plants, and the potpourri of colours, is refreshingly cheerful. Far from creating a museum-like garden for visitors, Xa Tollemache has composed a lively design which reconnects with the past. As might be expected, she is also planning for the future. Beyond the Walled Garden, over the moat on the far side of the shelter belt, she has started planting what will become a small arboretum. The trees are nothing more than slender saplings as yet, but at Helmingham there is no real rush and it is far more important that they root well and gradually adapt to the conditions. The arboretum will have clearings here and there, and small rises and dips in the lay of the land. Lady Tollemache is particularly proud of this aspect of her work, for ever since her appearances at Chelsea, where she watched the digger drivers in awe of their earth-moving skills, she has wanted to do the same. She now holds a certificate to drive a digger and can sculpt the earth herself.

WILD FLOWERS

Following on from the young arboretum, at the top end of the garden is a little-used tennis court surrounded by an apple orchard full of cowslips and orchids. This wildflower meadow is one of Xa's newer projects and her contribution to extending the garden in a natural way. From here, a path parallel to the moat leads on to an Apple Tree Walk planted by Xa 'because we are in the country.' This low-key feature forms an effective transition into the sweeping and more exposed parkland. As we wandered down the Apple Tree Walk, Xa drew my attention to the ancient espaliered fruit trees trained against one outer wall of the Walled Garden. Anyone wanting to take a closer look can cross a small wooden bridge conveniently constructed halfway down the moat. The puzzling matter as to why

The warm glow of dahlias, mellow sunflowers and *Verbena bonariensis* underplanted with French marigolds (*Tagetes patula*), is in harmony with the soft colours of the house.

the garden should ever have been surrounded by water can perhaps be explained by the number of animal bones found buried deep in the soil; the area was probably a stockade with safe pasture for cattle, dating back to a time when livestock had to be protected from marauding aggressors.

The past is tangible at Helmingham, through the house, the family's ancestry and the landscape itself. Xa Tollemache is not alone in having devoted herself to the garden; it seems that the men of Helmingham have a knack for finding wives who fit in perfectly and make the garden their life's work. A book entitled *The Tollemache Book of Secrets*, a complete facsimile of a manuscript held in the hall's library, was published in 2002 by Lord Tollemache in his capacity as member of the Roxburghe Club (the oldest society of bibliophiles in the world). It reveals much about life in the fifteenth and sixteenth centuries. Beside Nicholas Bollard's text, which includes instructions on planting herbs and a set of drawings for knot gardens, Catherine Tollemache's *Recipes of Pastry, Confectionery etc.* is of particular interest. Compiled between 1580 and 1612, during her time as lady of Helmingham Hall, Catherine's book deals with far more than cookery: it contains instructions for herbal remedies, perfume-making, cleaning clothes and gardening.

LITERARY INSPIRATION

The Book of Secrets provided the inspiration for the smaller second garden, on the opposite side of the main house to the Walled Garden. When Mollie Salisbury (better known as the Dowager Marchioness of Salisbury, an outstanding plantswoman who created two exceptional gardens, at Hatfield House in Hertfordshire and Cranborne Manor in Dorset) happened to be visiting Helmingham Hall, she remarked that a knot garden would be a perfect addition. The historical plans contained in the book were consulted and a design drawn up. Today it is hard to imagine that the Knot Garden, so at home in its surround of dense yew hedge, was created as recently as 1982 (see picture on page 116). Standing on the 'mainland', across the moat from the hall, it is a perfect counterbalance to the larger Walled Garden. As Xa points out, there

was nothing here before apart from her father-in-law John, 4th Lord Tollemache's collection of ornamental ducks, which had free range.

The success of the Knot Garden is due both to its scale and how it has been incorporated into its setting. Whereas the Marchioness of Salisbury at Hatfield House created an extensive and quite magnificent knot with a complicated pattern befitting the grandeur of her house, Helmingham Hall's version is more modest and suited to its rural location. It has been paired with a four-square pattern interplanted with herbs, and beyond lies a Rose Garden, all forming a wonderfully coherent unit when seen from the upper storey of the house. While two of the beds in the Rose Garden are filled with rosa mundi (*Rosa gallica* 'Versicolor') and R. 'The Fairy', underplanted with forget-me-knots (*Myosotis*) and edged with catmint (*Nepeta racemosa* 'Walker's Low'), others are planted with Portland, Bourbon and David Austin roses. The romantic atmosphere is heightened in spring by the blossom of a huge cherry tree standing in the adjoining swimming-pool garden. This, and the

Some of these plants, including box, *Iris* 'Sable', delphiniums and white lavender (*Lavandula* x *intermedia* 'Alba'), came from one of Lady Tollemache's exhibits at the Chelsea Flower Show and have been given a new lease of life here at Helmingham.

The ornamental gourd walk: each of the metal tunnels extending across the Walled Garden has been planted differently, adding character and variety to the garden.

Sweet peas (*Lathyrus odoratus*) are undervalued and due for a revival. The combination of scented flowers with the George Carter seat at the end of this vista is particularly charming.

shady, wilder part of the garden around a small pond nearby, are the family's favourite spots. Sheltered from the wind, they serve as a private retreat when the gardens are open to the public.

The developments seen at Helmingham gardens in recent decades resemble a labyrinth, cleverly flowing from one part to the next. An avenue of snow pear trees (*Pyrus nivalis*) with a low edging of box, leads to the coach house. Underfoot is a path of decorative brick paving, with occasional spaces left for herbaceous plants to fill. Touches of this kind add to the harmony of the overall picture, which is overlaid by an elegant modesty. Lady Tollemache's favourite spot is the fire pit – clear evidence of her practical approach. In a similar vein, when she felt she lacked the skills to get her design ideas down on paper, she opted for a course on technical drawing rather than garden design. She has come a long way since taking those fledgling steps many years ago, and has made herself a name as both a garden designer and a highly respected plantswoman. She was elected on to the council of the Royal Horticultural Society in 2013, serves on several RHS committees and is a Garden Advisor at RHS Hyde Hall in Essex. She cites Rousham in Oxfordshire, Hidcote Manor in Gloucestershire and Rosemoor, the Devon RHS garden, as places that have inspired her. All have a mixture of the picturesque and romantic, which permeate the garden even to the smallest areas. There is a strong sense at Helmingham that the past is cherished and no matter how much the outside world might change the Tollemaches will preserve and embellish this very special garden.

GUIDING PRINCIPLES

❈ A hunger to learn more about gardening and continually add to one's knowledge.

❈ Formal areas are in the vicinity of the house and the further one moves away the more natural the design and planting become.

❈ The emphasis is on having fun with colour and – to a lesser extent – a willingness to experiment.

❈ It is vital to draw inspiration from the past.

SIGNATURE PLANTS

❈ Roses such as *Rosa* 'Debutante' (4th image from top). The full palette of old and new roses is used to form the floral backbone of the garden, not in a formal manner but in a more relaxed and romantic way.

❈ Peonies.

❈ Irises, including *Iris* 'White City' (1st image from top), I. 'The Citadel' (2nd image from top) and I. 'Sable' (3rd image from top).

❈ Box (*Buxus sempervirens*) and yew (*Taxus baccata*) for hedging, cones and domes.

❈ Wild flowers, as Lady Tollemache remarks, because they are 'decorative in the transition areas and exciting, as you never know what is coming'.

' The past is tangible at Helmingham, through the house, the family's ancestry and the landscape itself. Xa Tollemache is not alone in having devoted herself to the garden; it seems that the men of Helmingham have a knack for finding wives who fit in perfectly and make the garden their life's work.'

RACHEL JAMES

FLOWERS BY THE SEA

How an abandoned farm became
a garden

Anyone visiting the exposed and remote landscape of the
Purbeck peninsula would hardly expect to come across a
flower-filled garden, and certainly not one as exceptional as
that created by Rachel James. Open fields stretch as far as
the eye can see and run right to the edge of the cliffs,
appearing to drop away into the sea. Green, blue and light
grey are the predominant colours on this outer boundary of
Dorset, where history is reflected in the names of its lanes
and fields. The fields are punctuated with numerous
small quarries where limestone has been excavated since
time immemorial. This is where the Jurassic Coast begins –

a UNESCO world heritage site – characterized by wonderful coastal formations. It is a region where harmony between the sea, landscape and craftsmen has prevailed for centuries.

Rachel James was brought up in Dorset, so later in life it was only natural for her to spend the summers on the coast with her young sons. In the 1980s, when the family began hunting for a holiday home, they were looking to buy a 'lock-up-and-leave' property which could simply be left to its own devices between visits. However, sometimes a place proves so irresistible that common sense is pushed out of the equation, as was the case with Eastington Farm, located on Dorset's Jurassic Coast. Thirty years ago, the adjectives 'rustic', 'quaint' and possibly 'hopeless' would have accurately described the property. The old farmhouse, a listed building dating from the sixteenth century, had been empty for years and was on the point of collapse. The landowner, the National Trust, had leased out the fields and was desperate to find someone interested in taking on this property and restoring it, along with the outbuildings, in a sensitive manner in line with the Trust's aim of safeguarding and preserving the coastline of England.

'Well, how could we say no,' recalls Rachel James with a smile, since Eastington Farm is a seductive combination of history, sea views and matchless character. For Rachel James and her husband Allan it marked the start of decades of construction work as one building after another was renovated or, if necessary, demolished. Each step along the way had to be approved by the appropriate conservation bodies, from English Heritage to the local planners, as well as the National Trust of course, as it was vital that the site retained its understated character within the landscape and remained recognizable as a farm. Crucial to the success of the project was the involvement of local craftsmen, who had a deep knowledge of the building materials and an almost instinctive feel for them. One of these skilled Dorset craftsmen, Jack Cobb, turned up every weekend for some ten years and, under the watchful eye of his dog, laid stone upon stone as he constructed new walls and repaired old ones.

For without this protective shield of dry-stone walls around the property, neither people nor plants would have stood a chance of survival against the wind.

SINGULAR ASH

As is often the case with farms in this sort of location, there was no garden to speak of. The site did, however, possess one major asset: there was a tree growing on the land, a rare phenomenon in a region where anything with an upright habit is flattened by the wind. Growing on the north side of the farmhouse and thus protected from the prevailing south-westerly winds, this magnificent ash (*Fraxinus excelsior*) with a low, broad crown seems – judging from its size – to feel happy here. It dominates the rectangular forecourt and whereas it used to be completely surrounded by an expanse of light-coloured gravel, it now stands in a generously proportioned circle of lawn. This was one of the first areas to be redesigned and marked the beginnings of the garden. Gravel has been used to cover the remaining surface, forming a turning circle and entrance to both the front and side door, but looks less harsh now that it occupies a smaller area and harmonizes well with the vegetation. Simplicity is the key to this area, with the tree and surrounding dry-stone walls defining the character of the place.

Walls divide up the land around and beyond the buildings, creating enclosures of varying size; despite their functional, even austere appearance, they have an undeniable aesthetic appeal of their own. And it is the walls that greet you at the gate. Flanking both sides of the drive, the parallel lines appear to squeeze the space, distorting its proportions and making the drive seem narrower and longer as it leads to the old farmyard. With the farmhouse to one side and the barns on the other, this area also appears larger than it is in reality. Narrow beds lining the walls are planted with an informal row of lacy, dark purple-leaved elder bushes (*Sambucus nigra*

'Black Lace'), bringing colour and animation. Adjacent to this, separated only by a wall, lies the nucleus of the garden, the forecourt around the ash tree. This is the best place to start a tour of the garden; and it soon becomes clear that you are in exceptional surroundings. Here, the light greys that have predominated up to now give way to lush greens and whites. The details are subtle, verging on the understated. A rose climbs up the house wall and domes of box flank the ancient oak door. More box topiary is scattered along the wall, lying like discarded buoys, with occasional white stone-like spheres in between providing an additional eye-catching feature. This interplay between traditional and contemporary, rural and architectural elements, is a theme repeated throughout the garden.

WALLED ENCLOSURES

Although not all the farm's outbuildings could be preserved, their outer walls were nevertheless left standing and now form different garden enclosures. Wandering through these spaces from one garden room to another is a joy. Eastington Farm was always intended as an addition to the James's London home, a place for the family to spend weekends and school holidays, so a tennis court was understandably high on the list of priorities. Hidden unobtrusively behind a high hedge, it is reached through a little garden filling the narrow space between the boundary wall and the outer wall of the old pigsty. Whereas the forecourt is cool and shaded, with a contemporary note, everything in this narrow flower garden is romantic, informal and awash with colour. Every shade of blue, pink and lilac is present in the clusters of catmint (*Nepeta*), different types of cranesbill (including *Geranium* 'Philippe Vapelle' and *Geranium phaeum* 'Samobor'), roses, *Allium aflatunense* and much more, all set against the background of a perfect lawn. A small side path runs from here to an opening, beyond which lies an absolute dream of a garden.

Dry-stone walls, the remnants of an old farm, run through the grounds and provide protection for plants such as *Rosa* 'Geranium'. Beyond the gap in the wall, the airy plumes of giant golden oats (*Stipa gigantea*) can be seen glowing in the sunshine.

The pond was part of the original farmyard, a reminder of the time when animals were brought here to drink. Now it is home to a family of ducks. The circular structure in the background is part of the Pool Garden, which like the walls was built using stone from local quarries.

Geranium × magnificum along with *G. clarkei* 'Kashmir White' and *G. pratense* 'Mrs Kendall Clark' make a fitting frame for the view. Along the path, making the most of a narrow space, is the Rose Garden.

The Pool Garden belongs in the pages of an upmarket glossy magazine. Enclosed by high dry-stone walls – the remnants of the old pigsty – the transformation of this space is amazing. You could easily mistake this for the Mediterranean, thanks to the tower-like circular stone building resembling an ancient Sardinian nuraghe, and aromatic planting that includes germander (*Teucrium chamaedrys*), thyme and slender Italian cypresses (*Cupressus sempervirens*). The beautifully constructed dry-stone tower is an artwork in itself, but it is more than just a feature as it houses all the equipment needed for the swimming pool.

DESIGN TOUCHES

As at Sissinghurst, some parts of the garden function as links between different areas. The transition from the informal flow of the flower garden to the more formal Rose Garden

is marked by a bronze statue. Gabrielle Peskin's *Venus of Kimmeridge Bay*, inspired by driftwood, stands sentinel at a pivotal point in the garden. Both on a visual and symbolic level this sculpture is absolutely appropriate, as Rachel's achievement in creating a garden in these difficult conditions is nothing short of an act of love. Prior to Eastington she was not a keen gardener; it was not that she was disinterested, but with two lively boys in tow she was simply too busy. It was only in the 1990s, when her children were older, that Rachel had time and was able to start thinking about the garden. It is easy to speculate, but one suspects that had she tackled the project earlier it might not have had the same self-assured flair, particularly in the way the spaces interconnect and flow.

Rachel's idea of siting a rose garden in the long, narrow but sunny space sandwiched between

Distinctive lollipop-shaped holm oaks (*Quercus ilex*), with an underplanting of *Iris* and *Allium*, divide up the large lawn.

the dry-stone wall in front of the tennis-court hedge and the long wall of the Pool Garden is pure genius. White and blue with a dash of yellow are the prevailing colours here. 'Macmillan Nurse' roses grown as standards – not 'Iceberg', as Rachel is quick to point out – line either side of the central cobblestone path. Rather than opting for a green background, of a hedge for example, as is so often the case in rose gardens, Rachel has kept with the limestone walls. A brave move, but the perfect foil for roses in a coastal garden. In this spot so close to the sea, colours appear intensely vibrant – an effect that calls for a bold approach. The Rose Garden acts like a corridor leading to the entrance drive, which seems, after the flourish of textures and colours, to be even more stark and monochrome.

Eastington's farmyard, reached along the drive, is not only surrounded by a cluster of buildings but is the site of a pond where livestock were once watered. Rachel and Allan thought long and hard about whether to fill in the irregularly shaped pond, but eventually decided not to because it is part of the farm's agricultural heritage. So the leaks were repaired, but no other improvement work was carried out. The pond's rustic charm contrasts beautifully with Rachel's contemporary planting along the side of the barn, where pollarded willows are underplanted with *Miscanthus sinensis* 'Gracillimus', golden oats (*Stipa gigantea*) and switch grass (*Panicum*), from which tall spikes of orange foxtail lilies (*Eremurus* × *isabellinus* 'Pinokkio'), Rachel's favourite plant, thrust skyward. The rationale for this extravagant planting is tied to the fact that Rachel has an uninterrupted view of this area from her bedroom window. Against the pale grey stone and the generally blue sky, the straw-yellow, rust-brown and orange of the planting stand out particularly well. The wind breathes life into this part of the garden and adds another dimension to it.

WALLED GARDEN

At this juncture in the garden it is hard to believe there is still more to come. But a door set into a high wall next to the house leads into a small walled garden with four square lavender beds enclosed by low clipped hedging, each with a conically shaped yew rising out of them as a central feature. The feel here is more formal than the rest of the garden, although the effect is softened in typical country style by delphiniums, lambs' tongue (*Stachys byzantina*) and climbing roses planted along the fringes of the house. Box had initially been used for the low hedges, but despite the sheltering walls they suffered from the constant salt-laden winds and have now been replaced with yew. It is astonishing that any plants can survive let alone flourish in such difficult conditions. Rachel's energy and tenacity are part of the miracle, and an example to any gardener working in similarly difficult conditions.

Friends understand why Rachel is so firm about the route they should take through the garden. For on the other side of a door in the far corner of this formal garden lies Rachel's pride and joy: an apple orchard that seamlessly flows into the surrounding landscape and is underplanted with a breathtaking sea of flowers. What an amazing blaze of colour – it feels like stepping into a painting by Claude Monet. Under a cornflower-blue sky, primary and secondary colours are splashed across the meadow: corn poppies (*Papaver rhoeas*), Icelandic poppies (*Papaver nudicaule*), cornflowers (*Centaurea cyanus*), love-in-a-mist (*Nigella damascena*), ox-eye daisies (*Leucanthemum vulgare*) and foxgloves (*Digitalis purpurea*) grow side by side in glorious, chaotic profusion. What is especially captivating, however, is the scene as a whole, best viewed from the elevated, fortress-like vantage point at the furthest extremity of the garden. The 360-degree panorama over the meadow bisected by the winding path and surrounded by countryside is magnificent.

The flower meadow was far from simple to create and was achieved only after a false start. The flowers planted first time round refused to grow, for unlike the rest of the garden with its poor, chalky, free-draining soil, the soil here is too fertile. This was once the vegetable garden and had been enriched with compost and manure for generations, making it excellent for potatoes but not for growing meadow flowers. Weeds grew fast, stifled the delicate wild flowers and the experiment was a failure. Removing the rich soil would have been too time-consuming and costly, so Rachel decided on a different tack, assisted by Malcolm, her gardener at the time, and his wife Liz. The area was cleared, leaving the old fruit trees in place, and left fallow for a year. In this way they were able to get the intrusive weeds under control. The following spring, a mixture of annual and biennial seeds was scattered directly over the soil, and as if by magic the desired effect was achieved. The meadow has to be recreated afresh every year: mown after flowering, cleared in October, sown the following spring and bursting with flowers by July.

DELPHINIUM TIME

Over the years Rachel has learned the various strengths of her remarkable garden. In the early days her efforts were based more on luck than design, but now she knows which plants have a good chance of thriving and which do not. Her confident use of colour developed over time and she has learned to employ it to best advantage.

It is somehow fitting that the newest part of the garden abuts one of the oldest. This area is more cautiously designed, for it was here that she learned first to battle and then to work with the elements. It is in this section of the garden that the shape of the old farmhouse becomes apparent; it comprises two wings at right angles, one jutting out towards the coast, the other more protected and enclosing the space, with a direct view of the coast. A broad band of flagstones follows the contours of the building, creating a generous patio. Mexican fleabane (*Erigeron karvinskianus*) has invaded the joints and appears to tumble over into the beds lining the edge of the lawn. Rachel's goal was to create an attractive setting for the house that consisted of

From the upper floor of the farmhouse, the sea appears to be a stone's throw away. This is an optical illusion, however, as the garden is separated from the sea by a field and cliffs.

This maze-like garden has many elements of surprise, not least the 'secret garden' behind this doorway. The sight of pink geraniums greets you, but across the threshold you discover that this is where Rachel grows her herbs.

more than lawn, and she has certainly achieved that. The picturesque house, perfect down to its window frames painted in subtly contrasting colours, now has the setting it deserves, one which also successfully integrates it with the broader landscape.

MARITIME CHALLENGE

Most people would have been more than happy simply to have a view of the sea, of fishing boats, yachts with white sails, and far off in the distance the tankers and container ships that daily cross the English Channel. On fine days, sky and water merge into a single, vast blue space which stands out sharply against the green of the fields. All the odds were against the planting of a garden in this exposed, wind-buffeted spot. But Rachel had other ideas: more than anything else, she wanted to tame the wind. And while she may not have tamed it altogether, she has adapted her gardening to withstand it. What gives the garden its edge is the interaction between the zesty colours of the planting schemes and the plain, dominant bulk of the walls. Each enhances the other in this innovative coastal garden.

GUIDING PRINCIPLES

❋ By using local materials, building techniques and the vernacular style of the area for walls, structures and paving, the garden is integrated into the surroundings and is not intrusive.

❋ Wind protection is essential in a coastal garden. Where it is not possible to plant windbreaks it helps, as at Eastington, to divide the garden up into sections that can be sheltered by walls instead.

❋ Buying plants from local nurseries has many advantages: not only are the plants adapted to local conditions, but as Rachel James discovered at Holme Farm Plants, Wareham, nursery owners are a good source of advice for novice gardeners.

❋ Make sure the garden looks good when seen from the windows of the house, so you can enjoy it without going outside in inclement weather.

SIGNATURE PLANTS

❋ The wildflower meadow in the apple orchard, including poppies (*Papaver rhoeas*) and ox-eye daisies (*Leucanthemum vulgare*) (top).

❋ Foxtail lilies such as orange *Eremurus × isabellinus* 'Cleopatra' (2nd image from top) planted with golden oats (*Stipa gigantea*).

❋ Bearded irises such as *Iris* 'Deep Black'.

❋ Pink-flowered Canary Island geranium (*Geranium palmatum* 3rd image from top) and cranesbills such as vivid purple-blue *Geranium × magnificum* (4th image from top, shown behind the upright spikes of lemon-yellow *Verbascum* 'Gainsborough').

❋ Evergreen architectural plants, such as box (*Buxus sempervirens*) and yew (*Taxus baccata*).

'"Well, how could we say no," recalls Rachel James with a smile. For Eastington Farm is a seductive combination of history, sea views and matchless character.'

THE HILLSIDE GARDEN OF SLEIGHT-HOLMEDALE

Where order and disorder reign
side by side

For anyone not accustomed to the stark landscape
of the North York Moors, it might seem unlikely that the
narrow country lanes running between dry-stone walls
could ever lead to the threshold of a beautiful garden. The
mighty expanse of heather moorland brings to mind the
Brontë sisters' novels *Jane Eyre* and *Wuthering Heights*,
driving rain and gloomy houses. On the approach to
Sleightholmedale, the avenue of maples with broad,
spreading crowns lining the road seems incongruous on a
hill otherwise sparsely populated with trees. The maples
peter out at the end into a patch of woodland that hugs the
slope and tumbles down into the valley.

In this region the landscape changes as quickly as the weather, as becomes clear the moment you peel off the main road and join the lane leading down to Sleightholmedale. The lane becomes increasingly narrower, steeper and more twisting as it descends into a meadow-lined valley with clusters of cattle and sheep. The scene appears even lusher against the backdrop of the bleak higher-lying moorland. Sleightholmedale, on the edge of the North York Moors National Park, is one of the most picturesque of Yorkshire's dales and it feels like a world apart.

With its long frontage punctuated by numerous gables and chimneys, Sleightholmedale Lodge is indisputably the lord of the valley. Nestled into the hillside, the south-facing, imposing yet homely building resembles a small hunting lodge and looks out over woodland which gives way to fields sloping down to the Hodge Beck river. The house was built in 1889 by Lord Feversham, whose main residence, Duncombe Park, was in nearby Helmsley. He gifted the estate, including a farm and associated buildings, as a wedding present to his daughter Lady Ulrica. Over a century has passed since then and Sleightholmedale Lodge is now in the hands of the fourth generation who live here and work the land. The house's future is ensured by an unusual family tradition whereby the estate is transferred to the next generation during the lifetime of the present incumbents rather then after their death. Just how the family finds time to garden in addition to running the farm is baffling, yet gardening is clearly in their blood. And besides, this is no ordinary family garden: it has opened its gates to the public for more than sixty years and is one of the jewels in the National Garden Scheme's crown.

UNIQUE ENCLOSURE

Unusual is the byword at Sleightholmedale. Nothing is quite as it seems, including the layout of the garden. There is no grand entrance, and at first sight it is not obvious where the garden ends and the landscape begins, as the two merge seamlessly together. It is only when you shift your attention away from the delightful house and start to explore that you realize why Sleightholmedale Lodge garden is so highly regarded, for here on the slope to the right, spread out over 0.4 hectares/1 acre between the building and the road above, is a garden like no other.

It is enclosed on just two sides by adjoining high brick walls, one fronting the road to the north and the other the wood to the west, creating an unorthodox semi-walled garden that opens up to the valley. But it is the way in which the levels have been mastered that really sets the garden apart. Rather than carving the hillside up into terraces, as is so often the case, it has been left as a single sloping plane. A grid of paths defines the garden's spaces, with rustic wooden trellises running parallel to them and serving to underscore the strong linear quality of the design. Three paths shoot down the slope, each interrupted at intervals by single steps, which act as both physical and visual brakes. The downhill paths are crossed in turn by three horizontal paths following the contours of the slope, one parallel to the top wall, one running through the middle of the garden and one near the bottom. This layout carves the garden into long, narrow borders along the perimeter and a cruciform of four large squares filled with flowers and crops.

The garden was designed over a two-year period by Lady Ulrica's husband, Brigadier General Everard Baring, after his return from India in 1905. During his time as military secretary to Lord Curzon, Viceroy of India, he would have encountered Islamic-style Mogul gardens as well as the hillside gardens of the country's cool, mountain stations. Both were to influence the design of his own garden, with which he laid the foundations of a passion that would be passed down the generations.

Judging by the beautiful paving to be found at intervals in the garden, Everard Baring was not interested in plants alone. The simple Yorkstone paths, contained within raised edging stones, are a perfect foil to the planting, while the three square patios positioned against the perimeter walls have an appealing aesthetic with echoes of Islamic gardens. Each is a variation on a theme: a diagonal cross paved in stone, infilled with bricks and completed either with a central stone square or rondel. One of the patios acts as a plinth for the summer house at the top of the central axis, and all three add incidental colour and shape to the garden, mirroring the texture of the brick walls. In the lower part of the semi-walled

The rockery, laid out by Rosanna's mother Helen Baring, with Scotch rose (*Rosa spinosissima*) in the foreground.

Paths rather than terraces subdivide the upper part of the semi-walled garden. The flower beds are large and impressive, and the plants appear to have a free rein.

garden, however, geometric paving serves a more prominent role as the central feature. Here, Baring placed a circle within a square, subdividing it into eight segments where planting alternated with brick paving laid in a herringbone pattern, revolving around an octagonal Yorkstone centre. Hybrid Tea roses once filled the beds but these have been replaced by perennials and annuals.

PLANTING FRAMEWORK

The formal structure of paths and trellis provides a valuable framework for the garden's exuberant planting. In the words of Rosanna James, Everard Baring's granddaughter and up until 2013 custodian of Sleightholmedale Lodge, 'l'ordre avec le désordre' (order and disorder) reign side by side here. This is an apt description, since the planting does not appear to follow conventional rules. Instead, there is a wonderfully dynamic mix-and-match approach in which perennials and roses are partnered with

a constantly changing selection of bedding plants and bulbs. There is also no deliberate policy of arranging plants by height, nor for that matter by colour; on these issues, happenstance takes the lead. Rosanna James has a particular penchant for annuals, which she uses to fill gaps between delphiniums, mullein (*Verbascum*), bellflowers (*Campanula*) and hollyhocks (*Alcea rosea*). While she does not stick to a defined colour scheme, as colour in itself is not of particular interest to her, it is vital in her view to know whether a plant will thrive in Sleightholmedale's harsh conditions at an altitude of 116m/380ft. Rosanna James is also constantly thinking about maintenance – after all, 0.4 hectares/1 acre of flowers and vegetables will not look after themselves – and on this subject she takes a pragmatic approach. As she explains, 'men of the land' rather than professional gardeners help tend the garden, which stretches beyond the semi-walled garden and covers a total of 1.2 hectares/3 acres. Retired

Rather like a firework display, this border is exploding with the colours of yellow mullein (*Verbascum*), purple hollyhocks (*Alcea rosea*), red crocosmia and a pink 'Hiawatha' rose over the pergola in the background.

blacksmith Bob Pettitt has turned out to be a gifted gardener and at over eighty years old is still propagating plants. Many plants are raised on site, making use of the existing stock and preserving old-fashioned varieties planted when the garden was first laid out.

DELPHINIUM TIME

Rosanna James keeps a watchful eye over everything and is actively involved herself. Her favourite time in the garden is the first week of July, before deadheading begins, when the delphiniums look glorious in front of the summer house. Among these, the cultivars grown by Rosanna James's grandfather are particularly pampered and cherished. So is the Wichurana rambling *Rosa* 'Minnehaha', introduced in 1905, with full, deep-pink blooms; and R. 'Hiawatha', a late-flowering single rose dating from 1904, with a white eye and ring of yellow stamens to its scarlet blooms. *Rosa* 'American Pillar' and

R. 'Albertine' also thrive here, festooning the timber trellises. Peter Beales rather than David Austin is Rosanna James's rose breeder of choice because their selections seem able to withstand Sleightholmedale's climatic conditions.

Continuity is as important in this garden as change, each generation adding their own touches without destroying the ambience of the whole. Rosanna James's mother, Helen Baring, made a significant contribution to the garden during her tenure, extending it to the east beyond the boundaries of her father's semi-walled garden. She built a terraced rockery in front of the house, and in the 1940s planted ornamental cherries in the sloping paddock next to the high garden walls, where she later added hundreds of narcissi. These have naturalized to form dense drifts, a magnificent display that vies for attention with the dainty canary-yellow flowered *Narcissus bulbocodium* along the path

The garden seems to flow seamlessly out into the bucolic landscape of the valley. Rosanna's award-winning cows are just as much a part of the scenery as the plants.

mown diagonally through the long grass up the slope. Here and there burst patches of bluebells, escapees from the neighbouring woodland, which enliven the scene and lend it an abstract quality. It is this mixture of naturalized and cultivated plants, together with the generous proportions of the garden, that is so captivating.

However, the best is yet to come. On the lower slopes below the semi-walled garden are carpets of scarlet *Tulipa sprengeri*, which have naturalized over the last fifty years. Rosanna James continues to take great care of these areas initially planted by her mother from just a few bulbs. She has also introduced some favourites of her own. About twenty-five years ago she was given a 'jumble' of seeds containing Himalayan blue poppies

(*Meconopsis grandis*), which naturalized and formed the beginnings of a remarkable collection. Now, in addition to intense blue, there are also purple, yellow and pink varieties of Himalayan poppy growing in the dappled shade beneath trees in the wilder sections of the lower slopes.

WILD PLANTS
As a young girl Rosanna James was already interested in wild plants. This early spark, together with the legacy left by her grandfather and the example set by her mother, have all influenced her work in the garden. She has a 'start again' list of areas that have got out of control, which helps her keep track of the work to be done in the next gardening year. Weeds are a terrible problem. They have been

Himalayan poppies are one of Rosanna James's passions. Here *Meconopsis grandis* mingle with aquilegias and the white pompoms of *Allium stipitatum* 'Mount Everest'.

The garden's spectacular show of colour begins on the lower slopes in late spring, with a rare display of naturalized *Tulipa sprengeri* interspersed with bluebells.

known to quite literally swamp her, and names such as enchanter's nightshade, dog's mercury, vetch and mare's tail roll off her tongue as if she had known them a lifetime. Only by radically clearing an area does Rosanna James stand a chance of gaining the upper hand. She has a no-nonsense approach to gardening and knows exactly what is suitable and what is not. She hates sculptures in the garden because 'why make a feature when the whole landscape is one?' Nor does Rosanna James pay any attention to trends. She simply does what she likes, how she likes, providing it is in keeping with the spirit of the garden.

As she herself concedes, she is fortunate in having a good eye for composition. The overall effect is far more important to her than the detail, as you might expect. Having grown up in the country, she has an innate feel for nature. She takes control with a gentle hand, works with what is already there and knows full well that gardens continue to develop. And because it is so important that the next generation has the chance to contribute, she recently handed over the reins to her son Patrick and his wife. Her young grandchildren will grow up surrounded by a wonderful garden and help keep the magic of this special place alive.

GUIDING PRINCIPLES

❊ Constantly think about care and maintenance.
❊ Seek help from farm workers capable of gardening instinctively and in tune with their surroundings.
❊ Focus on the overall effect.
❊ Try to raise as many plants as possible on site, as they will usually be more robust than nursery-bought stock.

SIGNATURE PLANTS

❊ Blue delphiniums, no matter what kind as long as they are hardy. Old cultivars from the turn of the twentieth century that have proved they are reliable include *Delphinium* Pacific hybrids (shown, top with *Rosa* 'Hiawatha' and 2nd image from top).
❊ Sea holly such as *Eryngium alpinum* 'Amethyst', shown with sneezeweed (*Helenium*, 3rd image from top).
❊ All varieties of Himalayan poppy, especially *Meconopsis napaulensis* (4th image from top).
❊ Annuals, which make excellent fillers and provide splashes of colour.

'Order and disorder reign side by side here. There is a wonderfully dynamic mix-and-match approach in which perennials and roses are partnered with a constantly changing selection of bedding plants and bulbs.'

SUE WHITTINGTON

A COUNTRY GARDEN IN LONDON

Sue Whittington's green paradise

In contrast to many other major European cities, London has grown over the centuries from a cluster of villages, all of which retain something of their individual character to this day. Places like Hampstead, Highgate and even Kensington have hidden corners that reach into the past and are home to some wonderful gardens, many lying concealed behind high walls. Step inside and you could easily forget that you are in the heart of a bustling city. However, certain gardens take you even further from the ordinary and everyday. Southwood Lodge, Sue Whittington's garden in North London, up on the hill in Highgate, is clear proof that English country gardens are not confined just to rural areas. Some of London's hidden gems open their gates to the public on certain days during the year in aid of the National Gardens Scheme (NGS), providing a rare opportunity for visitors to peek behind the scenes. Since the organization was founded in 1927, the number of participating gardens has risen from 609 to around 4,000. Many are relatively small private gardens, but world-famous sites such as Sissinghurst, in Kent, and Great Dixter, in East Sussex, also take part in the scheme in order to raise money for charity. It was usual in the early days of the NGS for the owner, very often the lady of the house, to be on hand to answer questions or serve tea and home-made cakes – a custom which still holds true today. For owners and visitors alike, these open days are an occasion to discuss problems and triumphs, exchange tips on where best to buy plants, and above all inspire one another.

The network of NGS-listed gardens is tightly knit, and the owners, like members of a club, are mutually supportive and more than willing to share advice. I came to hear about Southwood Lodge during a visit to a wonderful little London garden not far from Regent's Park. Lucy Gent, the owner and herself an accomplished gardener, told me that Southwood Lodge was an absolute must and should be on my list of gardens to visit. She also mentioned that it had been created by Sue Whittington, who happened to be the woman responsible for selecting NGS open gardens in this part of North London. There could not be a higher recommendation, and so it was that a year later I arranged to visit with a group of gardening enthusiasts. On arriving in Highgate Village, which is very much within the boundaries of London, it felt as if we had indeed stepped into a village. Even the 1960s housing development clinging to the slope next to Southwood Lodge had picked up on the leafy character of the area. Sue Whittington's garden is shielded by high walls, giving passers-by no indication of the paradise tucked away here, and the ground on which it stands is unusually steep. Highgate is situated on a ridge, the North

Every plant on the terrace is straining to be seen, including greater quaking grass (*Briza maxima*) with delicate *Clematis* 'Arabella', and opposite them an edging of frothy *Alchemilla mollis*.

All the paths in the garden are used to best advantage: here *Phygelius aequalis* 'Apricot Trumpet', white roses and *Clematis* 'Arabella' form a pleasing combination in front of purple-leaved berberis.

London Heights, on the edge of the large expanse of open green space that makes up Hampstead Heath. Considering that this part of London was originally a distinct village, it is somehow fitting that Sue Whittington's creation should have all the qualities of a flower-filled country garden.

ARCHITECTURAL MERIT

Southwood Lodge is a detached town house dating from the early nineteenth century. It appears unremarkable from the street, as if it had turned its back on the outside world. From within the courtyard, however, this grade-II listed building reveals its true architectural merit. For while the roadside elevation is bland, the other three sides of the lodge are distinguished by long sash windows in elegant Georgian proportions. The authentic character of the house was saved by restoration work that reversed alterations made in the 1960s, when the building was being used as an old people's home. The facade had been marred by the random addition of a series of bay windows, and half the roof had been lifted to squeeze in

an extra storey. The surrounding garden was at that time extensive but neglected – there was virtually no trace of its former Edwardian splendour, only suggestions in the position of the trees of how it might have been. Most of the site was sold off for the award-winning 1967 Kingsley Place housing development designed by the Architects Co-partnership, and only a fraction of the original garden remained attached to Southwood Lodge.

Sue Whittington has been gardening here since 1978 and knows her terrain inside out. As she points out, though, it was the previous owners who were responsible for the basic structure of the 0.1-hectare/⅓-acre garden, which she then took over and developed. When she and her husband Christopher acquired Southwood Lodge, the house had already been returned to its original design by a far-sighted and courageous architect. The extensions had been torn down, walled-up windows reopened and the Georgian symmetry of the building restored. The garden had also been improved.

Plants seem to sprout from every crack, even clothing the steps leading through a gap in the beech hedge up towards the terrace by the house.

A sunny seating area next to the house is enveloped in greenery, and the brick walls have been cleverly camouflaged by a hornbeam hedge clipped into arches.

The terrace and beech hedging stem from this time – the latter, as a visitor to an NGS open day proudly related, had been brought along as a gift in plastic carrier bags. Looking at the hedge, now standing at over 4m/12ft in height, it is hard to imagine that this space-defining feature was ever a row of tiny seedlings. The couple who took over Southwood Lodge from the architect likewise added their contribution to the garden. According to Sue, the lady of the house was particularly blessed with a talent for gardening. Sadly, she was not as fortunate in her marriage and when she and her husband parted company after seven years they were obliged to sell the property. Thus it was that Sue and her husband came to buy this beautiful house, and it only takes a brief glimpse of the garden to see how settled the present owners feel here.

CAPTIVATING BEAUTY

Despite her modesty, Sue's own contribution to the garden should not be underestimated. Even on windy, ice-cold winter mornings, the garden glows with a captivating beauty. Sue Whittington understands and loves her plants, those she has inherited as well as her numerous additions. Listening to her talk about the different types of pruning required by each tree and how difficult it is to resist new plants, one cannot fail to appreciate her affinity with the place. She gained her first taste of gardening in 1969 after moving into a fifteenth-century cottage near Stowmarket, Suffolk, but more because it simply needed doing than out of a desire to create a garden. There followed a period spent in the USA, where an enthusiastic friend introduced her to the joys of vegetable-growing. Over time she developed a passion for ornamental plants and well and truly got the gardening bug. In 1984 she completed a course at the English Gardening School, which at the time was located within the Chelsea Physic Garden, beside the Thames. It was here that Sue extended her knowledge of garden design, in particular the importance of getting ideas down on paper and drawing a plan to scale. She also realized that although major projects first had to be worked out in theory, a great deal of the detail could actually be decided on site. As a result, the garden at Southwood Lodge, while

Sue knows how to frame a vista. A statue beckons the visitor through the beech hedge and down into a more formal enclosure with the feel of a green theatre (also pictured on page 150).

having a distinct structure, is filled to the brim with plants, as dense as a jungle in places. Sue's role models include Sissinghurst and Hidcote Manor Garden, Gloucestershire, not to mention Lucy Gent's garden nearby in Gloucester Crescent, Camden. She describes her creation as a plant-lover's garden, where the boundaries between the formal and natural are blurred, and fate is allowed to play its part. She does not sink into despair if a plant dies but sees it as an opportunity to plant something new. In the strip between the greenhouse and the house is Sue's mini-nursery, with row upon row of plants that she has raised and is waiting to pop into the next free space, or to offer for sale on open days. There are also the 'plants I have known and loved', those that were not quite right and have been sent to the graveyard.

UNFOLDING DESIGN

One of the special qualities of the garden at Southwood Lodge is the way it gradually unfolds like a good piece of music, leading from an introduction into a middle section and finale, interspersed with well-spaced crescendos. The entrance courtyard, which is also used for parking and the garage exit, is surrounded on all sides by high walls. Climbers and various plants in containers brighten this area and prevent it feeling bare. From here, only a narrow opening in a corner of the courtyard suggests that the garden continues. Following through, you arrive at a terrace where every free space is lavishly packed with plants in colourful profusion. The effect is one of ordered chaos, and the contrast with the courtyard could hardly be greater. During summer pelargoniums in every shade of red, from deepest magenta to vivid tomato, are grouped in pots around the slender white pillars of the portico at the entrance to the house. On the semicircular steps clumps of Mexican fleabane (*Erigeron karvinskianus*) and tiny bellflowers (*Campanula porscharskyana*) spring from between the cracks. The stone paving has likewise been invaded by small plants. Negotiating them is like walking across stepping stones, one's eyes constantly on the ground. This focus on the plants has the effect of softening the formality of the terrace.

Four equally-sized square beds appear to envelop the seating area in the centre and initially divert attention from the main lines of sight. With the towering beech hedge on one side and the high brick wall of the garage in the right-hand corner, this feels like a separate little garden in itself, tempting the visitor to linger.

The classic facade of Southwood Lodge looks all the more elegant against the lush planting of the terrace. The house is situated on the highest part of the grounds, from where the garden drops away in two directions, to the east and south. Clever use of vistas is one of the garden's strengths and creates a memorable experience. From the terrace there is a long view artfully framed by an arrangement of ornamental shrubs and specimen trees. In the distance, a church tower is just visible and there is a suggestion of buildings and treetops. Standing here at 115m/377ft above sea level, it is amusing to think that there is no higher point between Southwood Lodge and the European continent – or, as Sue puts it, 'nothing between here and the Urals'.

Before descending the slope to explore beyond the terrace, an intriguing glimpse through an archway in the beech hedge calls for investigation. Steps aligned on an axis with the main entrance of the house take you under a tunnel covered with evergreen *Clematis armandii* down to a statue set in a niche originally of *Pyracantha*. Because this became leggy, undisciplined and significantly encroached on the narrow space, it has been replaced with yew, which Sue can keep in better check. Although still young, as it grows taller the new hedge will give this space, with its carpet of lawn, the aura of a green theatre. Shapes rather than colours play the starring role here, and the rather formal style of this thin strip of garden at the foot of the retaining wall is offset by quirky details such as edging the beds in alternating box cones and balls which diminish in size the further down the slope they go. The foliage-covered walls are also worth a second glance, the most delightful feature being the magical, if modest, *Clematis* 'Alba Luxurians' with its green and white flowers.

The sense of being far removed from the metropolis intensifies as you penetrate further into the garden and enter the 'wilderness', also referred to as the 'fairy dell', which begins where the terrace wall ends. Descending steeply, the garden becomes narrower, the shrubs appear to grow more densely and the suspense of not knowing what to expect grows stronger. Shade-loving plants provide ground cover and little paths lead away from the lawn – one winds around a mighty solitary conifer and then up the slope on the eastern side before turning back on itself and meandering down again like a stream. There are many exciting plants to admire, but your attention is irresistibly drawn to the small metal seat by the pool. This quiet, contemplative spot, right at the end of the garden by the boundary wall, is like a box at the theatre: sitting here, you can pause to enjoy a superb view of the expertly planted slope. The various greens of the foliage are punctuated by touches of variegation, a subtle and utterly beguiling combination of shades which gain in impact by being planted together. Purple-leaved *Cercis canadensis* 'Forest Pansy', glossy *Prunus lusitanica* 'Variegata' and the pale splashes of small-leaved *Pittosporum tenuifolium* 'Tandara Gold' provide wonderful highlights. Interspersed among these are self-seeded yews clipped by Sue into various amusing shapes – here a lollipop, there a slender column. The wilderness also harbours a stream, a relic of the old Edwardian garden, which trickles into little pools and over waterfalls created in stone, to be swallowed up by lush vegetation somewhere around the seat. The narrow trails crossing the slope, barely more than beaten paths, were originally made of grass; but when this eventually proved impractical Sue decided to add granite setts, thereby introducing a more contemporary touch to the garden.

The contribution made by light and shade in a garden is often underestimated, but at Southwood Lodge not only does the play of light create an additional visual dimension but

Seasonal change is important in a garden. After the tulips have finished flowering, it is time for the pelargoniums to be brought out of the greenhouse and take their place around the portico.

different light levels also provide a variety of habitats and a chance to introduce a broader spectrum of plants. Shade-casting plants play an important role, including shrubs such as Chilean myrtle (*Luma apiculata*) with its striking cinnamon-coloured bark. Their dappled shade is ideal for underplanting with hostas, peonies, cranesbills such as *Geranium* 'Brookside' and *G. phaeum*, Solomon's seal (*Polygonatum* × *hybridum*) and *Ranunculus aconitifolius* 'Flore Pleno'. Another notable element in the garden's appearance is provided by the many multi-stemmed ornamental shrubs planted individually or in groups. The effect of their twisting, dark bare stems against the green-cloaked slope is otherworldly.

FAVOURITE MOMENTS

Spring and early evening are Sue's favourite moments outdoors, while the new greenhouse, the hub of the garden, is her favourite spot in bad weather. Victorian in style but equipped with up-to-date facilities such as a rainwater butt located under the work surface, the greenhouse was erected to replace a more modern structure. Sue afterwards found out that the design she happened to choose was absolutely in keeping with the turn-of-the-century greenhouse originally sited here. It is this natural gift and confidence in her choice of plants and other features that have contributed to making Southwood Lodge an exceptional garden. Sue's instinctive feel for what is right and what is not, her ability to learn from mistakes and her determination not to be diverted by trends come from decades of familiarity with her subject. What Sue Whittington has achieved above all is to have imprinted her individual style on the garden while working with and respecting its existing features. The garden does not belong to any particular era, is neither voguish or nostalgic, but it could not be more ideally suited to its spectacular location.

GUIDING PRINCIPLES

❋ Work with what is already in the garden and capitalize on the existing topography.

❋ Thin and trim multi-branching shrubs to let light in and to create gaps which allow glimpses of views.

❋ Accept the hand of fate and embrace new opportunities.

❋ Construct a greenhouse, essential for overwintering pot plants, raising new plants from seeds and cuttings – and daydreaming.

❋ Have the courage to introduce a breath of fresh air into the garden by making occasional changes.

SIGNATURE PLANTS

❋ *Daphne bholua* 'Jacqueline Postill'.

❋ *Paeonia delavayi*.

❋ Tulips such as *Tulipa* 'Ronaldo' and 'Prinses Irene' (top image).

❋ *Rosa* 'Sally Holmes' (2nd image from top), seen here with Himalayan indigo (*Indigofera heterantha* syn. *I. gerardiana*).

❋ Many rare and exotic treasures, such as the exquisite Argentine creeper *Iochroma australe* (syn. *Acnistus australis*) (3rd image from top), which is unfortunately not frost-hardy.

❋ Various types of clematis, including *Clematis* × *durandii* (4th image from top, here set against *Pittosporum tenuifolium* 'Tandara Gold').

'Sue does not sink into despair if a plant dies but sees it as an opportunity to plant something new.'

RINGING THE CHANGES

Helen Dillon's surprising town garden

The Irish counties of Cork, Waterford and Wicklow, and the Dublin area in particular, have seen the emergence of several outstanding new gardens. Leading the way is Helen Dillon's influential garden in Sandford Terrace, central Dublin. What sets her garden apart is its fresh approach, dynamic feel and the wealth of ideas that keep it from standing still. The 0.3- hectare/¾-acre plot has been continually evolving since it was first laid out in 1973, and is still capable of surprising and delighting visitors. Helen Dillon has been tending plants for more than seventy years, ever since she was given her first primulas as a child growing up in Scotland. She has made a name for herself on both sides of the Atlantic, gives talks, works untiringly in her garden, is always receptive to new ideas and is not afraid of change. Awarded the Veitch Memorial Medal by the Royal Horticultural Society in 1999, an honour which placed her within the inner circle of England's gardening world, Helen Dillon could easily have left it at that. Her garden was considered to be the epitome of a romantic plant-filled haven. Surrounding an immaculate central lawn were mixed borders where rare plants collected on overseas expeditions grew cheek by jowl with traditional herbaceous perennials. Beyond the lawn, a semicircle of arches covered in ivy and clematis framed a circular pool with an antique 'wedding cake' fountain in the middle, creating an eye-catching feature at the end of a central vista. Hidden behind the arches was another flower-filled garden room, adorned with a charming sculpture of the goddess Diana. The north-facing front garden was equally well designed, with a curved path leading to the front door between gently sloping beds brimming with plants. Having opened to the public in the early 1990s, the garden was admired, applauded and declared a paradise.

EVER-CHANGING TAPESTRY

However, a garden is no museum: it evolves and is never completely finished. Plants get moved around. New ideas are brought in. And number 45 Sandford Road is no exception. In 1985, inspired by a visit to Morocco, Helen Dillon made the first in a series of changes that astonished friends and visitors – she removed the fountain, thereby converting the pool into a circle of still water. About ten years later it was the front garden's turn. Helen Dillon felt the house deserved a better setting to enhance its classical Georgian facade. 'A house needs to sit down,' is how she puts it. Acting on the advice of a friend, landscape architect Feargus McGarvey, she had a retaining wall built parallel to the driveway, steps added and a large area by the front door paved in sandstone. The house now had a dignified entrance. And whereas cars had previously been in full view of the kitchen window, they were now hidden by the wall.

No sooner had fans of the garden got used to these changes than the next round was underway. Helen Dillon had been writing a column for the Irish *Sunday Tribune* since 1992, in which she discussed the garden's ups and downs. Readers knew and grew attached to the garden, even identifying so closely with it that they perceived it to be in some way theirs. Many, including certain garden aficionados, were horrified when it was redesigned in 2000. The central lawn was completely removed and replaced by a long rectangular pool, flanked on either side by a wide band of silver-grey Irish granite paving. The existing circular pool, surrounded by stone setts, was integrated into the design and the borders substantially widened. Towards the house, the broad garden steps bridging the level changes between the lower ground floor and the garden were reconfigured and divided into two narrower flights of steps with a cascade in between. The only remnants of the old garden were two sphinxes on either side of the steps, which still stand guard over the dynamic new design. These radical changes were partly due to Rosemary Verey (see page 60), who had visited Helen's garden while on a lecture tour of Ireland in the 1980s and commented that the lawn might benefit from a central rill. Subsequent trips to India and Spain, in particular to the Alhambra's famous Myrtle Courtyard, helped reinforce this idea in Helen's mind. A major drawback of the central lawn had been how it seemed to swallow light, making the surroundings duller and robbing the planting of some of its brilliance. By contrast, sheets of water are light-enhancing, illuminating overcast days.

Helen's husband Val compares her garden to a stage with a large cast of extras in the form of 'movable' plants in containers. Waiting in the wings are lilies, dahlias, *Alstroemeria* and many others planted in ordinary black plastic pots and metal dustbins, which are unobtrusive and do not compete visually with the plants. 'What I love is the impermanence of container gardening,' says

Helen. 'Bought yet another plant? Can't think where to put it? Simple: buy another pot. With containers a whole new universe is revealed … If you don't like last year's creation never do it again.' The theatrical effect is particularly evident from the drawing room on the raised ground floor. Seen from this perspective, the garden appears to be far longer than its 54m/177ft, due not only to the central canal but also to the open nature of the site. Aside from an old apple tree, all the trees placed judiciously around the garden are smaller-growing, including a beautiful paperbark maple (*Acer griseum*) and pinnate-leaved *Aralia*.

Colour is one of the most striking aspects of the garden. As Helen Dillon explains, before the changes of 2000 took place the garden's colour scheme was based on a palette of pastels 'that everyone has had for a hundred years'. Following a visit to Metz in France, where Helen admired the pretty, silvery municipal flower displays, she decided to switch to a colour scheme resembling an 'over-painted picture with a bit of blue thrown in'. The finished effect

was to look like a packet of Smarties, zinging with primary and secondary candy colours. So, the border on the left of the canal is now reserved mainly for reds and oranges, while the one on the right is predominantly blue and white. As befits her motto 'don't be afraid of orange', Helen has a succession of different plants on display in this glowing colour. *Alstroemeria* fell out of fashion long ago but has been restored to acceptability by Helen's use of it as a filler in the hot bed. Opposite, cool shades are provided by bellflowers (*Campanula*), white valerian (*Centranthus ruber* 'Albus') and noble delphiniums, which are cut back after flowering to bloom again from early July into August. Helen is always ready to try a new species even if it ends in tears, as was the case with agave-like *Furcraea parmentieri*. For despite the mild winters and a protective covering, this precious plant did not survive, proving that even an experienced gardener can still learn a thing or two.

Trial and error is a hallmark of this garden, as is a willingness to adapt and incorporate new ideas.

Helen Dillon is a passionate plant collector. Pictured here is rare *Kniphofia thomsonii* var. *thomsonii* and yellow *Verbascum* 'Frosted Gold', with the distinctive wands of a white-flowered *Dierama* behind.

Miss Willmott's
ghost (*Eryngium
giganteum*) and
striking marsh
orchids
(*Dactylorhiza* ×
braunii) grow in
the dappled shade
of an apple tree
and *Rhus typhina*.

Inspired by a scene encountered when travelling by train from Moscow to Berlin, Helen Dillon decided to plant birch trees in her front garden: an unusual prelude to a truly inspiring garden.

In 2005 the front garden underwent another makeover, the sandstone paving replaced by larger slabs of light grey Chinese granite and the planting completely altered. Inspired by a three-day train journey between Moscow and Berlin during which Helen travelled through birch woods, she decided to plant a stand of filigree *Betula* 'Fascination' underplanted with angel's fishing rods (*Dierama*) and ornamental grasses such as *Stipa tenuissima*.

Although Helen Dillon yearns for 'virgin' soil, hers is a long-established garden with soil that has been worked for over a century. She does her best to replenish it by bringing in tons of cow manure; not particularly elegant, perhaps, but essential if the plants are to flourish. That this is a private garden and not simply for show is also evident from the small vegetable patches casually tucked in behind the delphiniums. As someone open to experiment, Helen remains willing to concede defeat but often opts for a change of tack. After the local fox had finished off the last of the hens, she gave up on that idea. Nowadays, the end of the garden is enlivened by the trilling song from an aviary of bright yellow canaries – the perfect touch in an eclectic garden.

Helen Dillon's garden does not conform to any particular trend and cannot be described as low-maintenance. Her short articles published monthly in *The Garden* magazine give a flavour of her informative, knowledgeable and witty style. Just like Vita Sackville-West, Helen Dillon writes from experience and from the heart, relating her knowledge and passion for plants. She is always receptive to fresh ideas. As she says of herself, 'I want to be a creator, not a curator.'

Overleaf
Helen has championed bright, zingy alstroemerias where others feared to tread.

GUIDING PRINCIPLES

* It is essential to understand the garden's basic conditions and be guided by them.
* Feed the soil, preferably with plenty of cow manure.
* Do not be squeamish if a plant is struggling: pull it out, send it to the compost heap and start afresh.
* Cultivate container plants in the greenhouse, then site outdoors to fill gaps.
* Ordinary metal dustbins or black plant pots are as good as expensive, eye-catching containers.
* Fish, blood and bone attracts foxes, which do a lot of damage digging up the soil. It is better to use rose fertilizer or even seaweed as an all-purpose plant food. A mycorrhizal (fungal) fertilizer is recommended, particularly for freshly planted roses or anything else that is struggling.
* How do you get rid of weeds? 'I pick them up between finger and thumb and put them in a bucket,' says Helen.
* Ensure plants are properly staked. At 45 Sandford Road, this task falls within Val Dillon's remit. He prefers semicircular metal rings with two prongs, as used by Margery Fish, and has them specially made by the blacksmith in sizes of 40cm/16in, 60cm/2ft and 90cm/3ft.

SIGNATURE PLANTS

* Sea hollies. *Eryngium* × *oliverianum* can live up to thirty years in the same soil and still be going strong. *Eryngium* × *zabelii* combines well with *Diascia personata* (top image).
* Colour accents, such as *Papaver somniferum* flowering among *Clematis* × *aromatica* (2nd image from top).
* Californian tree poppy (*Romneya coulteri* 3rd image from top).
* Angel's fishing rods in variety, including *Dierama* 'Blue Belle' (unfortunately not frost-hardy and needing to be overwintered indoors, 4th image from top).
* Alstroemeria, once popular as a floral decoration for the dining table, deserves a more prominent place in the garden. Opt for taller varieties and grow them in pots, as these plants have a tendency to spread quickly.

'What I love is the impermanence of container gardening. Bought yet another plant?
Can't think where to put it? Simple: buy another pot. With containers a whole new universe is revealed ... If you don't like last year's creation never do it again.'
Helen Dillon

BIBLIOGRAPHY

Beth Chatto

The Dry Garden, Dent, 1978

The Damp Garden, Dent, 1982

The Green Tapestry: Perennial Plants for the Garden, Collins, 1989

and Christopher Lloyd, *Dear Friend and Gardener: Letters on Life and Gardening*, Frances Lincoln, 1998, new edition 2013

Beth Chatto's Gravel Garden: Drought-Resistant Planting Through the Year, Frances Lincoln, 2000

Beth Chatto's Woodland Garden: Shade-Loving Plants for Year-Round Interest, Cassell Illustrated, 2002

and Fergus Garrett, *A Year in the Life of Beth Chatto's Gardens*, Frances Lincoln, 2011

Helen Dillon

Helen Dillon on Gardening, Town House, 1998

Helen Dillon's Garden Book, Frances Lincoln, 2007

Margery Fish

We Made a Garden, Collingridge, 1956

An All the Year Garden, Collingridge, 1958

Cottage Garden Flowers, Collingridge, 1961

Gardening in the Shade, Collingridge, 1964

Ground Cover Plants, Collingridge, 1964

A Flower for Every Day, Studio Vista, 1965

Carefree Gardening, Collingridge, 1966

Gardening on Clay and Lime, David & Charles, 1970

Gertrude Jekyll

Wood and Garden, Longmans, 1899

Home and Garden, Longmans, 1900

Lilies for English Gardens: A Guide for Amateurs, Country Life, 1901

Wall and Water Gardens, Country Life, 1901

and Edward Mawley, *Roses for English Gardens*, Country Life, 1902

Flower Decoration in the House, Country Life, 1907

Children and Gardens, Country Life, 1908

Colour in the Flower Garden, Country Life, 1908

and Sir Lawrence Weaver, *Gardens for Small Country Houses*, Country Life, 1912

Annuals and Biennials, Country Life, 1916

and Christopher Hussey, *Garden Ornament*, Country Life, 1918

Mary Keen

The Garden Border Book, Viking, 1987

and Clay Perry, *The Glory of the English Garden*, Barrie & Jenkins, 1989

Colour Your Garden: A Portfolio of Inventive Planting Schemes, Conran Octopus,1991

Decorate Your Garden: Affordable ideas and Ornaments for Small Gardens, Conran Octopus, 1993

Creating a Garden, Conran Octopus, 1996

Vita Sackville-West

Some Flowers, Cobden-Sanderson, 1937

In Your Garden, Michael Joseph, 1951

In Your Garden Again, Michael Joseph, 1953

More for Your Garden, Michael Joseph, 1955

Even More for Your Garden, Michael Joseph, 1958

Rosemary Verey

and Alvilde Lees-Milne, *The Englishwoman's Garden*, Chatto & Windus, 1980

The Scented Garden, Michael Joseph, 1981

and Alvide Lees-Milne, *The Englishman's Garden*, Allen Lane/ Penguin Books, 1982

Classic Garden Design: Adapting and Recreating Garden Features of the Past, Viking/Penguin Books, 1984

and Alvide Lees-Milne, *The New Englishwoman's Garden*, Chatto & Windus, 1987

The Garden in Winter, Frances Lincoln, 1988

Good Planting, Frances Lincoln, 1990

A Countrywoman's Notes, Frances Lincoln, 1991

Rosemary Verey's Garden Plans, Frances Lincoln, 1993

Rosemary Verey's Making of a Garden, Frances Lincoln, 1995

The English Country Garden, BBC Books, 1996

Rosamund Wallinger

Gertrude Jekyll's Lost Garden, Garden Art Press, 2000

Gertrude Jekyll: Her Art Restored at Upton Grey, Antique Collectors' Club, 2013

OTHER WORKS

Jane Brown
Vita's Other World: A Gardening Biography of Vita Sackville-West, Viking, 1985

Ursula Buchan
Garden People: Valerie Finnis and the Golden Age of Gardening, Thames & Hudson, 2007

Timothy Clark
Margery Fish's Country Gardening, David & Charles, 1989

Victoria Glendinning
Vita: The Life of Vita Sackville-West, Wiedenfeld and Nicolson, 1983

Jeremy Griffiths & A.S.G. Edwards,
The Tollemache Book of Secrets, The Roxburghe Club, 2001

Anne Scott-James
Sissinghurst: The Making of a Garden, Michael Joseph, 1974

Francis Jekyll *Gertrude Jekyll: A Memoir*, Jonathan Cape, 1934

Ursula Maddy
Waterperry: A Dream Fulfilled, Merlin, 1990

Russell Page
The Education of a Gardener, William Collins Sons, 1962

Barbara Paul Robinson
Rosemary Verey: The Life and Lessons of a Legendary Gardener, David R. Godine, 2012

ADDRESSES

The Beth Chatto Gardens
Elmstead Market, Colchester, Essex CO7 7DB, UK
www.bethchatto.co.uk

East Lambrook Manor Gardens
South Petherton, Somerset TA13 5HH, UK
www.eastlambrook.com

The Dillon Garden
45 Sandford Terrace, Ranelagh, Dublin 6, Ireland
www.dillongarden.com

Helmingham Hall Gardens
Helmingham, Stowmarket, Suffolk IP14 6EF, UK
www.helmingham.com

Kiftsgate Court Gardens
Chipping Campden, Gloucestershire GL55 6LN, UK
www.kiftsgate.co.uk

Sissinghurst Castle
Biddenden Road, near Cranbrook, Kent TN17 2AB, UK
www.nationaltrust.org.uk/sissinghurst-castle

The Manor House
Upton Grey, Hampshire RG25 2RD, UK
www.gertrudejekyllgarden.co.uk

Waterperry Gardens
Near Wheatley, Oxfordshire OX33 1JZ, UK
www.waterperrygardens.co.uk

Gardens open occasionally, often as participants in the National Gardens Scheme (www.ngs.org.uk):

Barnsley House
Barnsley, Cirencester, Gloucestershire GL7 5EE
www.barnsleyhouse.com

The Old Rectory
Duntisbourne Rouse, Gloucestershire GL7 7AP

Sleightholmedale Lodge
Fadmoor, Yorkshire YO62 7JG

Southwood Lodge
33 Kingsley Place, Highgate, London N6 5EA

IMPRINT

Frances Lincoln Limited
74–77 White Lion Street
London N1 9PF
www.franceslincoln.com

First Ladies of Gardening
Pioneers, Designers and Dreamers
Copyright © Frances Lincoln Limited 2015
Translation by First Edition Translations

Original Edition Callwey 2014
Copyright © 2014 Verlag Georg D.W. Callwey
GmbH & Co. KG
Streitfeldstraße 35, 81673 München
www.callwey.de

All photos with the exception of historical
illustrations © Marianne Majerus, London

A catalogue record for this book is available
from the British Library.

ISBN 9-780-7112-3643-1

Printed and bound in China

1 2 3 4 5 6 7 8 9

ACKNOWLEDGEMENTS

*Without all the hard work on the part of the
garden owners, including the National Trust
at Sissinghurst, and their willingness to be
out in their gardens whatever the weather, these
outstanding gardens would not exist. We would
therefore like to thank them all for permission
to photograph and publicize their gardens.
Our thanks go to Beth Chatto, Mary Keen,
Helen Dillon, Xa Tollemache, Anne Chambers,
Rosamund Wallinger, Gill Richardson, Rachel
James, Sue Whittington and Rosanna James.
We are also grateful to Mike Werkmeister of
East Lambrook Manor Gardens, as well as
Richard Gatenby, Head Gardener at Barnsley
House and Rob Jacobs, Garden Manager of
Waterperry Gardens, who took the time to talk to
us. Special thanks go to the team at Waterperry
Gardens, for granting us access to historical
photos. We would also like to thank the librarians
of the Royal Horticultural Society's Lindley
Library, who retrieved from the archives the
literature we needed for our research.*